■

"I'm on *The Soul Diet*. This rigorous program works on the deepest levels of humanness. It allowed me to disconnect from the clutter of daily patterns and examine the beauty of my journey. It is a process of recovery. I'm a journalist—a working member of the media—so the Media Fast was an authentic challenge. The ability to disconnect and focus on reality continues to bring me joy. *The Soul Diet* brings one to a still, beautiful place. In those peaceful surroundings, an authentic joy and meaningful focus can be found. *The Soul Diet* is so much more than a simple, how-to guide. It is an exacting map that allows one a way to discover purpose, joy and fulfillment. The process is demanding and beautiful."

Eric Slocum
Emmy award-winning broadcast journalist at KOMO 1000 News

"This well-written book presents a new approach to self-development: one based on genuine insight and one that takes effort to practice. This honesty is refreshing; in a world of quick-fix superficial self-help material, it shines through."

Akiva Tatz, MD
author of *Anatomy of a Search* and *Letters to a Buddhist Jew*

"Beautifully written, clear and compelling, *The Soul Diet* is an important wake up call for everyone who wants to lead a richer and more meaningful life."

Laura Leibman
Associate Professor of English and Humanities, Reed College, Portland

"An insightful in-depth erudite book on soul searching in a complex world."

Ron Kenner
former Metro staff writer for *The Los Angeles Times*

THE
SOUL DIET

THE
SOUL DIET

Ten Steps Towards Metaphysical Health

Yitzchak Goldman

Neeman House Publishers, LLC
Seattle, Washington

First Neeman House Edition
Copyright © 2007 by Yitzchak Goldman

ISBN 10   0-9779899-0-9
ISBN 13   978-0-9779899-0-4

Publisher's Cataloging-in-Publication
(Provided by Quality Books, Inc.)

Goldman, Yitzchak.
The soul diet : ten steps towards metaphysical health
/ Yitzchak Goldman.
p. cm.
Includes bibliographical references.
ISBN 0-9779899-0-9

1. Religious life. 2. Soul.   I. Title.

BL624.G6348 2007   204'.4
QBI06-600194

Printed in India
10 9 8 7 6 5 4 3 2 1
Edited by Ron Kenner, rkedit.com
Cover and layout design by Lisa Moore, Lari Power
Author photo by Sara Simon
Production coordinated by Edward and Nancy Starkman

Attention colleges and universities, corporations and spiritual living/ health organizations:
Quantity discounts are available on bulk purchases of this book for educational purposes, premiums or gifts.
For information contact Marketing Department, Neeman House Publishers, 5135 South Garden Street, Seattle, WA 98118.

Acknowledgments

This book and the entire *Soul Diet* concept would have remained mere hypothesis were it not for the unstinting support and encouragement of my wife, Sara. To our young children who are easily wowed by the number of words dad can type on his computer, you are all my joy for living. A very big thank you to my editor Ron Kenner, who through both selflessness and creativity managed to sharpen my words without losing my message. Thank you also to his wife, Mary and to Tom Puckett for their supporting editorial roles. Laura Leibman's proofreading skills proved to be invaluable. Thank you, Laura.

To Lisa Moore, the exceptionally diligent cover and interior layout designer for *The Soul Diet*, I am very grateful for your ability to envision exactly what I imagined and to transform that into reality. Thank you also to Lari Power for her design input and to the following individuals for their contributions at various stages of the manuscript development: Rabbi Dr. Akiva Tatz, Dr. Irwin Schiller, Stuart Kaufman, Tabatha Werblud, Ian Wiener, Sam Fleishman, Shirley Edelstone and David Klinghoffer. I am also indebted to the Seattle Kollel for their continuous support and understanding.

Beware of cute little blurbs
At the beginning of a book

– Anonymous

Table of Contents

1. Orientation   **15**

What This Book is Not   15
The Right Fit   16
A Dictionary Definition, Please   16
Confronting Yourself   17
The Power to Create and Destroy   18

2. Why a Soul diet?   **21**

Food for Thought   21
Clarity vs. Clutter   22
Spiritual Junk Food   25
Follow Your Heart? My Foot!   26
The Resolution   27
Eh… Where *Are* We Headed?   28

3. Wait a minute. Just what is the soul anyway?   **31**

Soulless Soul   31
The Nefesh   33
The Neshamah   33
The Good Conflict   35

4. Step 1: The Media Fast   **37**

Spouse for Life   37
What's the Big Deal?   37
TV or Not TV – Is There Really a Question?   37
As Seen on TV   39
Newspapers and Other Print Media   42
Catch the Eye or Die   43
Small Talk   44
Ronnie from Reno and Nuclear Energy   44

Beauty and the Beast 46
So What, Exactly, Do You Mean By a Media Fast? 49
Email 50
When to Begin the Fast 50
Should I Do Each of These 10 Steps One at a Time? 50
Withdrawal Symptoms 51

5. Step 2: Schedule Slimming **53**

Noise, Please 53
Cocooning 54
Duty Free or Free of Duty? 55
The Greener Grass Syndrome 56
How Do I Coordinate This Period Together with the Media Fast? ... 58

6. Step 3: The Ledger **59**

Inner Surgery 59
The Seven Categories 60
The Common Denominator 61
Mechanism 62
Regression 64
Trampled By the Elephant 65
Willpower 65
Willpower Insider Information 66

7. Step 4: Order and Fitness **69**

Fueling Up First 69
It's Not the Diet, It's the Conviction 71
Recommendations from Maimonides 74
Order, Outside and In 76
Unhealthy Fitness, Unhealthy Order 78
It's About Time 79
Fill-in 81

8. Step 5: Anger Control **85**

Playing Anger Geography 85
Self-worship 86
Visiting Their Heads 89
Tunneling with Talk 90
I Can't Stand It 91
Angerless Anger 93
Fill-in 94

9. Step 6: Speech Control   **97**

       Words Do Break Bones   97
       Cosmic Power   98
       Gossip and Slander   100
       The Truth about Lies   101
       Fill-in   102

10. Step 7: The Giving Factor   **105**

       The JFK Principle   105
       Magical Mechanics   106
       The Give and Take of Taking   109
       Fill-in   111

11. Step 8: Intimacy   **115**

       Vision from Outer Space   115
       The Power of Intimacy   116
       Today's Pornography is Tomorrow's Art   118
       The Subtleties, Wink, Wink, Nudge, Nudge   120
       Fences Are the Best Defense   122
       Fill-in   124

12. Step 9: Goal Control   **127**

       Worth the Wait   127
       Mental Cardiology   131
       The Goals   131
       Follow-through   132
       Fill-in   133

13. Step 10: The Happy Factor   **135**

       The Sitcom Syndrome   135
       The Freedom Trap   137
       A New Angle on Depression   139
       Activate!   140
       Fill-in   142

14. After the diet   **145**

       Appendix I   **151**

       Appendix Ii   **155**

       Bibliography   **171**

1

Orientation

What This Book is Not

THIS IS NOT A "FEEL GOOD" BOOK. If you're looking for a momentary lift, a collection of inspiring quotes that make you smile as you sit by the fire, warming your heart as you warm your feet, then... this is *not* the book for you.

This book is upfront and direct. The style caters to those interested in a frank exploration of the soul and metaphysical health so that certain goals outlined here can be achieved. This may seem confrontational as some of the contents will challenge conventional wisdom and your own personal world view.

However you interpret the tone, the intention is solely to carve a path to clarity. Those truly in search of clarity will be strong enough to endure the rocky road on which this book will lead them. Inevitably there will be those who find themselves on the defensive. I welcome your comments and your challenges.[1]

If you still do want that instant fuzzy feeling you get from a golden sunset or a teary movie on the Hallmark Channel, please put this book down and pick up some achiever's story of hope and inspiration that leads him or her to resounding happiness and success in life; a story you can read while on your treadmill burning calories. And after you turn off the treadmill you can take the message with you forever, or perhaps for the next day or two before you pick up the next achiever's book for your treadmill.

This book seeks to avoid the quick fix, the cosmetic solution that looks good yet does not penetrate; merely fades as quickly as it comes. What I am trying to say, if not yet clear, is that unfortunately our society tends toward the superficial thrill to satisfy spiritual thirst; a sensation that tickles you pink, makes you gush, cry, and clench your fists into iron-willed champions as you chant, "Yeah, yeah—I can do it," all the while spurred on by friends and family as cheering spectators whispering in your ear, "I believe in you. I believe in you...."

Meanwhile, of course, you haven't much changed your life at all.

---

[1]See full contact information on page 174.

The Right Fit

Let me tell you a secret—I know how that sounds, but just give me a chance. This is something you've long known about yet perhaps haven't clearly articulated: *Genuine spiritual contentment does not come in a party packet.* You cannot buy such contentment off the shelves, no matter how much you are willing to pay. You cannot do it in your spare time on the subway to work. You cannot take a class in it once a week for an hour. You cannot reserve it for a special occasion such as sitting around a cozy campfire, eyes searching the stars. Nor can you condense it into bright and glossy bumper stickers that champion your enlightenment.

A fleeting indulgence on your part in an undemanding, neatly tailored spiritual experience may have its appeal; but on closer inspection you'll discover that all you have accomplished is squeezing some aspect of spirituality into your schedule. Your daily life remains dominated by your normal essential activities; your spiritual life is a minor adventure on the side. Even if inspiring, motivating and enervating, your spirituality remains an outside source that you sometimes tap into. The bottom line: your spirituality is convenient because it doesn't much interfere with your life.

The Soul Diet is going to expect you to let spirituality interfere with your life. *You will no longer try to fit spirituality into your life, you will try to fit your life into spirituality.* I know this book is slim and that there are limits to its scope, but I will try to create a personal guide to the monumental task of real spiritual change, the kind of change – a transformation to metaphysical health – that helps you fit your life into spirituality.

A Dictionary Definition, Please

What exactly is metaphysical health? Well, it's one of those definitions that takes a book to explain. We'd have to tackle the basics first before gaining a comprehensive understanding of metaphysical health. We'd need to define the soul and what it means to go on a Soul Diet. We'd need to understand what is detrimental to the soul and what elevates the soul. We'd need to understand how our character traits influence the soul, and how our approach to internal battles and challenges shape the soul. Such elements require serious investigation and this book pursues that objective. Not exactly a piece of cake. *But* if you're standing on one leg and would like a telegram-definition of metaphysical health we could, before going any further, describe it as follows:

> *The process of eliminating clutter in order to make the right choices.*

Since such a telegram might seem vague to you now, I recommend standing on both legs so that we can explore metaphysical health more thoroughly. And thorough it's going to be, with the proverbial blood, sweat and tears and a few gasps thrown in for good measure. I know I am beginning to sound like a drill sergeant, yet I also realize that even if it requires some hard work there are people reading this text who are sufficiently disillusioned with the standard party-packet spirituality favors that they are eager to ditch these candies for a more profound guide to change.

By the way, on your hunt for true spirituality, bear in mind that any doctrine that seems so easy and comfortable that it snuggles right into your life probably belongs to the party packet, like those emails you get about making millions while working at home.

One hopes that some of us are a little wiser now about such promises. Making millions has never been easy and never will be. Of course it's not impossible to make millions, but there's no easy alternative to hard work. It's inevitable.

Similarly, this program requires commitment and serious effort toward effecting change. You are not going to get away with calling your mystic in the morning and taking, as directed, two spiritual tablets.

Thus, once again, if you think this sounds too harsh, too heavy or too holistic for you, please put the book down. I know that doesn't do much for my marketing strategy but I really do want the right kind of person to be reading this book. You have to be ready to go on The Soul Diet.

Confronting Yourself

The essence of the change you will encounter in this book is internal. Part of being ready to go on the diet is the willingness to take the plunge and confront your inner self head on. This is a mighty but doable—challenge. If there's something lacking or wrong inside us, it is near instinctual to ascribe this to outside factors:

- The reason I get angry often is because people provoke me.
- The reason I have this empty feeling inside is because nobody or nothing around me inspires me.
- The reason I lack willpower is because my parents did not educate or discipline me properly.
- The reason I am dissatisfied in life is because I don't have enough money.
- The reason I have been unsuccessful in life is because nothing has gone my way.

As the years pass, our faulty reasoning evolves into the undisputed truth, curious ideas pretty much at home in the contours of our minds. As long as we don't shine a spotlight on this illusionary thinking it will by and large escape scrutiny, nestling there quite content with the status quo. That is why an attempt to brush away the cobwebs and stare ourselves down is commonly met with resistance and even panic. In fact we are often deathly afraid – I am not exaggerating – of facing ourselves head on. It calls for a scrupulous evaluation of our character and generally we run for cover rather than stand to the test.

Thus Rabbi Yisroel Salanter[2], the famous progenitor of an ethical movement called *Mussar*, declared it more difficult to change one character trait than to learn the entire Talmud.

---

[2] Rabbi Yisroel Lipkin of Salant (1809–1883).

This brings me to another essential point in introducing this book:

As a rabbi, most of my sources are Torah based, culled from the ancient authoritative commentaries as well as the contemporary ones. Some sources listed in the footnotes are available only in Hebrew since they are for a very specialized market. Some are even printed in a special style of text that differs from the modern Hebrew standard. Thus most of what I am saying is not my own thought; I just happened to collate the material in a format accessible to the average reader, Jew or non-Jew. Although the material is Torah-based, the wisdom imparted in this book is suitable for people of all creeds or caliber. This book will not require you to do anything typically Jewish; you will not even be expected to eat bagels and lox every Sunday morning.

So, now I will try to answer some questions and reservations that may be swimming around in your head:

Q: What if I don't know what the Torah is?

A: It doesn't matter. Even after reading this book, you won't know what the Torah is. (Does that comfort you?) Just take the information and use it.

Q: But what if I don't believe in the Torah or even in God?

A: OK, a little more complex. Put it this way: If you are 100% sure that you don't believe in it, how will you ever trust my sources? So, again, put this book down. This is the third time I have told you to do it. Listen to me already! If, however, you rate yourself as less than 100% sure that you don't believe in it, then you have nothing to lose by reading on.

Q: What if I want to convert to Judaism after reading this book?

A: Please, don't be ridiculous.

The Power to Create and Destroy

As noted, this program is directed to people of all walks of life. What makes it so universal? What all people in the world share is that they are created in the Divine Image. Now what does that mean? Some insight is provided by the *Nefesh HaChaim*.[3] (Don't worry about trying to pronounce these words. Of course, that's probably like telling you not to think about pink elephants.)

Being created in the Divine Image means that we are all endowed with a microcosm of God's capabilities. Even though we are by no means infinite or omniscient, there is a miniscule element of God's capabilities programmed inside us. Just as God has the power to create and to destroy, so, too, on a much smaller scale, we have the power to create and to destroy, both through action and through speech.[4] This concept requires clarification. When I say we have the power to create, I am

---

[3] Literally *The Soul of Life*, a classic philosophical work written by Rabbi Chaim of Volozhin (1749–1821).

[4] The subject of speech is a principle element in this program and is given fuller treatment in chapter 9.

not necessarily referring to fulfilling any dream that pops into our head. Sometimes fulfilling our dreams is actually destructive, not creative.

If you think, for example, that the power to create means the drive to make millions of dollars, the thought is not necessarily true for many possible reasons. If a sixteen hour day is required to make those millions (so that your family will eventually be better off?) that could do considerably more damage than you imagine. Children who have a "customer service" relationship with their parents i.e. "have a good day" and "have a good night," have suffered more than any amount of money can make up for. What is viewed as creative, therefore, can effectively be destructive. Thus, we introduce the concept of not letting our hearts lead us down the garden path, which we will develop further in the next chapter.

Discretion and guidance are needed to help us evaluate the truly creative and the truly destructive. The right kind of creativity elevates the soul. The wrong kind degrades the soul. As you make your way through this book, you will notice that this insight forms the broader basis for all the various steps you'll need to get closer to metaphysical health. Although the steps seem unique and independent of each other, in actuality they are all expressions of one underlying theme—making sure you choose the right kind of creativity. You will discover that *The Soul Diet* will direct you along the path of the right kind of creativity so that your soul is elevated—not degraded—through your actions. You will discover how this diet provides you with breathtaking clarity, an unprecedented bird's-eye-view of your self and your challenges. With this book you will take great pleasure in rising above the confusion wrought by contemporary pseudo-wisdom. You will learn how to gain the confidence to know what's right for you, to know what's good for you, and to know what direction you need to take. Above all you will learn how to maintain and sustain this level of clarity in your everyday life, no matter what happens. Yes, it is a long and challenging path but the reward is certainly immeasurable.

2

Why a Soul Diet?

IF YOU ASKED SOMEBODY TO DEFINE *DIET*, most likely, within their first few words, they would mention "food." Or "calories." Or the words, "leave me alone." Whatever their response, dieting is almost unanimously described as the control or restriction of food intake.[1] Diet programs are a multibillion dollar industry, an enormously popular subject to talk about, write about, and establish societies upon. Revolutionary weight loss ideas are spun one after another at an amazingly fast rate, all capturing the attention of the public and all promising incredible results. And many of them deliver. Thus if you are at a party and raise the subject of a diet, any diet, you will generally open up a Pandora's box of comments, figures, facts and comparisons. Sometimes a particular diet becomes so popular that you are classified as either being "on it" or "not yet on it." An outsider might get a little nervous observing this little cultural phenomenon, hoping that he or she is not relegated as being "not with it" for not being "on it."

Now what if you were at that same party and you boasted to the crowd that you were on *The Soul Diet?* The conversation might die down for a few seconds, perhaps out of confusion but mostly out of awkwardness because your turn of phrase may have identified you as one of those fringe people to be avoided if at all possible. Maybe the guy next to you asks if *The Soul Diet* has something to do with fish. You answer, "no," and he is afraid to ask any further.

Dieting, as we commonly understand it, addresses only the physical side of our existence. Today's world, in particular, places tremendous importance on frequent exercise and limitation of certain foods with the goal of achieving a healthy, trim, and attractive body. In truth there is an additional, often more fundamental, diet that is glaringly ignored: the need to control our intake of things that are not good for our souls.

So much of the population is physically healthy. How much of the population is metaphysically healthy? A person who exercises for an hour every day, who is meticulous about what and how much he eats, and who subscribes regularly to health and nutritional publications, can still be totally unfit when it comes to his spiritual health.

---

[1] Merriam-Webster defines dieting as
  1: to cause to take food
  2: to cause to eat and drink sparingly or according to prescribed rules.

Clarity vs. Clutter

Clutter is the first symptom of the problem. Over-indulgence is definitely not limited to food. It applies also to our sensory world. Some may be aware of this and others not, but our lives are cluttered with sensory objects, images, and feelings to the extent that we can't see the forest from the silicone trees. Clutter is a fundamental problem. Technology, cultural metamorphosis and new age wisdom have reached unprecedented levels of innovation and presence in our world. While most look at these developments as moving in the right direction, as carving a path towards an enlightened human race, few realize the disorienting effect it has on us. Culture critic Neil Postman classifies those who embrace the technology without any concern as "Technophiles."[2] It is dangerous, he argues, to view technology exclusively as a blessing without any accompanying burdens.

Clutter is the New Age burden. In our every day lives we come into contact with so many images, ideas, desires, choices and ideologies that, instead of a feeling of increased freedom, we have lost total clarity of who we are. The bombardment of images is so virulent that it has become increasingly difficult to grab our attention, much like the effect that overuse of antibiotics has on our body's immune system. And we can't keep our attention, either. Our minds switch to the next image, and we very quickly forget the previous one.

I don't have to tell you that wherever you look, you will be surrounded by at least one of the following:

- The ring of your cell-phone
- An SMS message on your cell-phone
- A string of billboards with a convincing finger pointed at you and your wallet
- 24-hour news coverage, 7 days a week, live, from every corner of the globe
- Uninterrupted political and social commentary sweeping all subjects and cultures blaring from your radio speakers
- Stock updates across your screen from markets around the world
- Spam email
- Junk snail mail
- Multilevel marketing schemes
- A myriad of discounts, specials, one-time offers, free samples
- The latest technological breakthroughs entering the market at breakneck speed
- Streaming videos, MP3 downloads, online chats, video conferencing, DVD's, DVR's, DSL....

---

[2] *Technopoly, The Surrender of Culture to Technology.* (New York: Vintage Books, 1993), 5.

The havens of peace and quiet are disappearing. Yes, there are people who object to the Federal Communication Commission's recent proposal to lift the ban on in-flight cell-phone use. But there are also people who complain that for two or three hours they have no contact with the world and insist that the ban be lifted. Even in taxicabs, where you can traditionally choose to be left to your own thoughts for a pensive fifteen minute ride, plans are under way to install wireless multimedia interactive systems so that you should not—not for one moment—loose touch with things.

As if that were not enough, we choose to fill our schedules so that every moment of our day is filled with something. Ever wonder where everyone was headed in the middle of the day on the freeway? Whether to a meeting of minds at Starbucks, a gathering of the underwater basket-weaving club, or to an out of town convention that debates whether life is static or dynamic, we are constantly on the move. We cannot allow a single moment of silence. Even when we get inside our cars it has become a reflex to turn on the radio. In other words, we, in collusion with society, are succeeding in drowning ourselves out.

In particular, we enjoy delving into the "issues" of the day. *Issues,* a highly likeable term, engenders an air of vital significance. On occasion there is a genuine need to debate the issues, but many times this focus represents nothing more than fluff; albeit elegant fluff with jargon so sophisticated that it can capture the hearts of the cultural elite. And it generally does not let go until the entire day is wasted. In some instances, entire lives are wasted on what seemed like crucial discussion but in reality withered with the arrival of the following day's newspaper.

Imagine that you are a commercial airline pilot seated in the cockpit, making your final checks before a long haul across the Atlantic. You introduce yourself to the co-pilot, and the conversation shifts to the previous day's political news.

"Oh, yeah. He doesn't stand a chance today in the primaries. I mean, as far as I'm concerned the race is over. I don't know why these guys who haven't even picked up any delegates keep it up even though they don't stand a chance."

Funny he's brought that up. You've been wondering the same thing. You sit back in your chair as if the cockpit is a cocktail lounge. "I don't know. These guys know they're losing but there's still thousands of people shaking their hands wanting their autographs. You still think you're wanted. Maybe it's got to do with denial, just not believing that it's over, or maybe it's tenacity, just hoping that something will happen to boost the campaign. Even with just one delegate they'd probably feel they're right back in the race."

The co-pilot raises his eyebrows. "That's interesting. You know, ever since I was a kid I've tended to be overly-optimistic about things. I remember once at a summer camp looking out my bungalow window, these like… big airy windows you know the kind that swept the whole length of the wall?…"

"Yeah. They don't make them like they used to." The co-pilot chuckles and shakes his head. The sunlight streams through the small jet windows.

"Yeah. Anyway so I was staring out at this really rough terrain…"

"Captain," the purser swiftly approaches you, "whenever you're ready…"

"Oh, I'm sorry," you say, slapping your side. "I suppose we'd better get on with this flight." You and the co-pilot chuckle. "I really need some sort of personal alarm system," you remark, disappointed with yourself. "I'm constantly getting side-tracked."

"What you need is an alarm on your PDA that integrates with your desk top," the co-pilot responds.

You consider this for a moment. "You're being serious?"

"Sure," he says. "When you HotSync to your PC, the information about your alarms is transmitted to a special compact application, which stores it and alerts you of impending events. Then you have a full personal information management system in itself, no matter where you are. And it always keeps you on track."

"Hmmm." You stroke your chin. "It gets updated on your PC automatically?"

"Well, yeah, I think it does an automatic save, but I'm not sure. I saw it in the business section of the paper last week. I think I can find it if I look for it."

"Is that where you get info on the latest software releases?" you inquire, thinking that you must subscribe to these things or you will keep on missing out.

"Yeah. And magazines, pamphlets. I keep an eye out here and there. I like the articles that give you an honest review of the product. You have to kind of separate the marketing hype from the reality." The co-pilot then gives a detailed comparative study of various publications that meet or deviate from his standards.

At the end of it you sigh. "I think it's time for me to get a new PC anyw…."

"Captain," the purser purses her lips. "Isn't it time for us to, you know, *fly?*"

"I'm sorry. You're right," you say, embarrassed, and turn to face your controls. "Boy, I think I need a coffee to get going here." You stop an attendant passing at the back. "Oh, could I get a coffee? I like to have something warm before we hit -55 degrees."

"Yes, captain. Would you like a large or small?"

"Uh…large is good."

"Sugar?"

"No. Sweetener."

"Sweet'n'Low, Equal or Splenda?"

"Splenda."

"One packet or two?"

"One is fine."

"Cream?"

"Well, I don't know. I presume the milk you have is homogenized, right?" Her stare is blank. She shrugs her shoulders. "I just read an article," you continue, "a very interesting one. You know you take these things for granted. I mean who thinks to worry about whether the milk is homogenized or not?" By her expression, you can see she has the same question. "Conventionally," you explain, "homogenization has been thought to be beneficial because it reduces fat particle size and therefore makes the fat more digestible. It also allows the fat particles to be evenly distributed throughout the milk and not rise to the top which requires milk to be shaken before it's served. But this article claims that the particles become so small that they pass through the walls of blood vessels and other tissues before they pass through the digestive system. That's scary, don't you think?"

The attendant tries to feign interest, arching her eyebrow. Even if the attendant is not as intrigued as you are, it does seem to have struck a nerve in the co-pilot. "One minute something is good for you and the next it's poison," he mutters. "Remember when you were a kid and they promoted milk like it was liquid gold? Gives you strength, calcium and everything?" You nod your head. "Yeah, and now they say it's bad for you. Even if you are not lactose intolerant. Boy, do I have a story for you about a case of lactose intolerance that went undiagno…"

"Captain!" the purser snaps, standing over you. "In the time we have wasted on the ground we could have been halfway across the Atlantic!" Her anger has clearly accelerated her heart-rate. "Now wait a minute," you protest, not quite able to face up to your recalcitrance. "We were not wasting time. We were talking about some very important issues. Do you think that updates on the election, on cutting edge software package releases and on nutritional health concerns are not critical of who we are and where we are going?" "We are going nowhere, captain," she responds dryly. "The voting count, PC alarms and fat particles aren't going to get you across the Atlantic."

Her way with words is perhaps superior to yours. She has a point. How easy it is to believe that we are going somewhere in life, rattling along the fast lane in a vehicle built from pseudo-issues, only to discover that our wheels are doing the "spinning but not touching the ground" thing.

Spiritual Junk Food

To make matters worse, the world purports to solve all the confusion created, by dishing out quick-fix solutions which are in reality just another symptom of the invasion and in effect serve to compound the clutter.

The Self-help phenomenon should be critically evaluated. There can be instances when the medicine becomes the virus. At times self-help books and workshops craft solutions that the reader wants to hear, not needs to hear. Very many of these books adopt a formula of identifying strengths, developing those strengths and putting them into action. That sounds great, but very few books will do the same for weaknesses, i.e. identifying weaknesses, working on those weaknesses, and correcting them for real life application. Why? Because it is far more appealing to believe there's nothing wrong with you, just that your greatness is waiting to be discovered; rather than face the fact that you do have things wrong with you and you should be doing something about them! Which of the following two books would you instinctively pick?

- *101 Ways to Bring Out the Winner Inside You*
- *101 Ways to Stop Being so Arrogant*

There may be a few readers who choose the latter, but the former is really the one where all the excitement is. Well, just as a juicy hamburger with fries is more enticing than a rice cracker with seaweed, there are attractive but unhealthy choices for our metaphysical tastes too. Providing solutions that steer around the problem may be comforting, and may lead you to think you're improving things, but in reality, they have added another layer to the clutter, further distancing you from the solution.

In addition, we are presented with nebulous, abstract philosophies spun by common culture to deal with the confusion. Sayings like, "life is what you make of it" and "true meaning is the joy we experience inside of us" have no grounding, do not define their parameters, and can actually (believe it or not) lead to the extreme detriment of the person following them. Let me illustrate further:

Follow Your Heart? My Foot!

We are all familiar with the inspiring words of wisdom uttered with boundless warmth, "Follow your heart, my child, follow your heart. Whatever you feel deep inside here (points to upper rib cage), that is what you should follow. Don't let anybody stop you, for you are master of your destiny, and what pulsates here (cups upper rib cage) is your guide to a happy and fulfilling life."

(Wind sweeps through hair against backdrop of setting sun, and violins reach crescendo.) Please, exit the scene. The first step in curtailing your intake is understanding that not every whim of your heart is good for you. Some of what your heart tells you is actually crippling.

Imagine the following scenario: A happily married man has a business dealing with a woman who has a certain way of stirring his heart. This feeling is very real for him and he begins to suspect that he never quite had the same feeling for his wife in all their years of marriage. This, despite the fact that he has never before questioned the viability of his marriage. This temporary pang can quickly develop into his adversary and before he knows it, it has destroyed his life and the life of his family.

> "Oh, that's different," you say. "Of course there are times that you should not follow your heart."
>
> And I say, what exactly determines when I should follow my heart and when I should not?
>
> "It's common sense," you respond, a little annoyed at my tendency to dissect everything.
>
> "Ah-hah!" I declare. "So you admit that reasoning is actually the primary force here, not the heart. Some sort of judgment on our part, our capacity for intellectual thought is the real director, determining whether or not our heart is right or not. The heart takes direction from the mind."

(And because I'm writing the book, I don't give you a chance to respond).[3] The Torah instructs us, "Do not spy after your heart and after your eyes."[4] *Rashi*[5] elaborates, "the heart and the eyes are spies for the body, procuring sins for it. The eye sees, the heart desires, and the body commits the sin."

If it is the mind that is the primary force, does that mean we should approach our decisions without any heart at all, *sans* emotion, like robots?

No. Of course we should experience our emotions. They should just be directed by reason. If your intellect approves a certain emotion, then by all means experience that emotion. Of course that requires a great deal of intellectual honesty. You cannot deceive yourself. You will be the one who loses out.

It also requires a tremendous amount of control. Difficult, but possible. The son of the revered Rabbi Moshe Feinstein[6] related that one of the most valuable qualities his father possessed was the ability to tune his heart to the moment at hand. Since Rabbi Feinstein was personally involved with so many of his students and colleagues, he would sometimes have to attend a funeral immediately after a wedding, and then attend another wedding right after that. At the weddings he would shine with pure happiness and joy. At the funerals he would sob bitterly. This ability to truly experience and switch emotions that were appropriate for the moment was one of his greatest virtues. Even though we can all relate to the difficulty of such a task, we should recognize that this is the ideal. Maybe one day we will get there.

The Resolution

That is why putting our hearts in check is a fundamental step in curtailing our intake. The more we can step back and take an objective view of our status quo, the better we will be able to evaluate ourselves with honesty. But as bold a move as it is, checking our hearts is not enough. We are inundated with so much clutter that we need a systemized diet plan to clear it all away.

The Sages provide an invaluable insight on the subject: *There is no happiness like the resolution of doubt.* This is because clearing the clutter will help us clear the confusion, and happiness is knowing for sure where we are headed, even if it entails hard work along the way.[7]

Professor Barry Schwartz of Swarthmore college, argues in his book, *The Paradox of Choice: Why more is less*,[8] that too many choices lead to anxiety, even depression.

---

[3] Actually you may respond with any comments and questions by referring to the contact section on page 179.

[4] Numbers (15,39).

[5] An acronym for Rabbi Shlomo Itzchaki, one of the principle commentators of the Torah. (1040–1105).

[6] Considered one of the leading Torah authorities of the past generation (1895–1986).

[7] We will discuss the concept of happiness in detail in chapter 13.

[8] Ecco. (New York: Harper Perennial, 2005). See Chapter 13.

In illustration of this, one could think of a diamond pendant resting on its blue velvet cushion. There is nothing on the cushion but the diamond. You cannot help but be drawn to the diamond. There is nothing obstructing your full appreciation of that diamond. Now what if you surround that diamond with zirconium, reasoning that filling the case with as much shiny minerals as possible will enhance your appreciation of the diamond? The truth is that the diamond now gets lost in the clutter and does not strike the eye as before.

This concept is not newly invented. The Hebrews received the Torah on Mount Sinai in desert surroundings. The Sages do not regard the desert location as merely circumstantial, as though the Hebrews happened to be there because they were on their way from Egypt to the land of Israel. On the contrary, the desert experience is understood to be a crucial component in the reception of the Torah. The desert represents barrenness and emptiness, devoid of all interference and clutter, both from a physical and personal point of view. In the desert, little exists but yourself. There are no accoutrements to your persona under which you can hide. Then, and only then, were the Hebrews ready to receive and to appreciate the Torah.

As for us in modern times, nothing has changed. As the *Midrash*[9] points out, "Whoever does not [nullify] themselves into a desert is not able to acquire wisdom."[10] Although this concept might make sense theoretically, it is uncommon to find people who have cleared the clutter and have conviction about their direction in life. It is equally uncommon to find people who are truly honest with themselves. However, to find people who have *both* conviction and honesty is a truly rare find. You won't find happier people than these. That is where we hope we are headed.

Eh – Where *Are* We Headed?

We are now about to do our groundwork before we start the diet. **In the following chapter**, we will seek a definition of soul before putting it on any diet. We will discover that there are actually two types of souls operating simultaneously inside us and that how we choose to deal with them determines our metaphysical health.

In **Chapter Four** we will start the diet with a two-week Media fast, and in **Chapter Five** we will be curtailing our schedules with a two week Schedule Slimming. Both these steps are designed to give ourselves a respite from the onslaught of imagery, ideas, and sound bytes preventing us from spending time with our own minds. As noted, they facilitate clearing the clutter clogging our souls.

In **Chapter Six**, when we are alone with our own thoughts, we will be introduced to a general ledger of the mind called *The Satellite Map*. This ledger enables us to commit to paper our successes and failures in dealing with our challenges. These challenges are categorized according to seven general themes, each the subject of the succeeding chapters of this book. The reader spends a week

---

[9] A collection of homiletical teachings of the Tannaic era (approximately 2000 years ago).

[10] Bamidbar Rabbah, Chapter 20.

focusing on each area of challenge. Thus in **Chapter Seven** the reader will spend a week dealing with Order and Fitness. In **Chapter Eight** we focus on Anger Control; in Chapter Nine, on Speech Control; in **Chapter Ten**, on the Giving Factor; in **Chapter Eleven**, on Intimacy; in **Chapter Twelve**, on Goal Control, and in **Chapter Thirteen**, on The Happy Factor.

The seven weeks of focus on our challenges are designed to help us sort out and separate thoughts, feelings ideas and actions, those which enable us to think in a healthy way, from those that contribute to our mental clutter. We will perform an inner surgery to remove some deeply embedded thought patterns, behaviors and defense mechanisms that we may have never questioned simply because we've have never truly given them any honest scrutiny. Just as a physical diet is designed to limit those excesses clogging our arteries, *The Soul Diet* is designed to limit those excesses clogging our souls.

The final chapter discusses our time after *The Soul Diet*: whether or not to repeat the diet and how to take the message of the diet with you for the rest of your life. This may seem like a tough program, but, as you will discover, removing the clutter is an exceptionally liberating experience. Someone who has completed *The Soul Diet* has completed an internal revolution that most people never experience. You will find your own honesty refreshing; you will find the insights you gain into your own mind and personality quite profound. Most of all, you will be a person of principle and of focus. You will not regret it.

3

Wait a minute.
Just what is the soul, anyway?

THE WORD 'SOUL' IS BANDIED ABOUT LIKE A DOLLAR BILL, taking on a broad variety of definitions ranging from the mystical to the musical. Some people describe it as the center of feeling. Some describe it as the center of consciousness. Some go beyond that to suggest it refers to that abstract, esoteric part of us that gives us meaning. Some say it refers simply to the physical life-force. Yet others say its realm is in legend.

I will share with you two examples in my own experience that really capture just how loosely and obscurely the word is defined. I passed a billboard on an arterial route that carried a large picture of Gandhi, and then the words below: "Soul. Pass it on." Very dramatic. Very moving. Very… ambiguous.

No doubt the creators of that billboard commercial assumed the public would get the gist of it. You know—*soul!* You all know what we mean, right? Another sight that got me thinking was the window of a trendy restaurant I was passing. The food offered was soul food, a specific type of cuisine developed by African Americans during their period of slavery. With nothing more than the scraps of meat and vegetables available to them to prepare nutritious meals for their families, they produced a simple yet stylish cuisine fashionable today. Here one could understand that the term 'soul' points to the people's *heart and soul* that they devoted to the creation of the food, typically under the most oppressive circumstances; even so, the term remains somewhat mystifying.

If the lay definition of the soul is obscure, then the professional definition seems profoundly so. The field of psychology is defined as the study (ology) of the soul (psyche). The derivation of the word "psyche" comes from Latin and the Greek "psuke," which is breath, life or soul.[1] If so, one would think then that psychology is precisely the field to answer all of our questions. Yes, the classical philosophers have mused at length about the soul, but this is a more specialized "diet book"—our aim being a practical guide to dealing with the soul. Thus we prefer to extract as

---

[1] Actually "breath" is the most accurate definition presented here when matched with the Torah's concept of soul, as you will see later on

rigorous and pragmatic a definition of soul as possible. You'd think that if psychology is the study of the soul, we'd find reams of detailed information about the soul developed over the centuries, archived in journals and other publications for all the world to see. Not so simple.

Because of the abstract nature of the soul, it has been almost instinctual, historically, to avoid the concept of the soul in psychological theory. Behaviorist theory, in fact, seems intent on defining psychology as studying only those behaviors that can be observed, almost quantitatively as a scientist would do. As behaviorist John Watson writes, "No one has ever touched a soul, or seen one in a test tube, or has in any way come into relationship with it as he has with other objects of his daily experience…. Why don't we make what we observe the real field of psychology? Let us limit ourselves to things that can be observed, and formulate laws concerning only those things."[2]

Thus the paradox emerges that psychology, the study of the soul, should avoid the study of the soul. Are we missing something here? As Carlton Cornett, L.C.S.W. points out, "Spirituality has been the unheard dimension in psychotherapy. Since spiritual issues form a major part of human life, it seems incredible that there would be resistance to the topic. Nevertheless, this resistance has a history almost as old as that of modern psychotherapy and a hold on current practice that is hard to loosen."[3]

A relatively new discipline, Transpersonal Psychological Movement, postulates an integration of a spiritual approach with traditional psychology. Brant Cortright describes it as "the melding of the wisdom of the world's spiritual traditions with the learning of modern psychology."[4] This is certainly a leap in the direction we're pursuing, but we are still left with a nagging problem: By embracing the notion of spirituality, Transpersonal Psychology seems to be opening itself up to vast, undefined territory. The concept of spirituality is so subjective, so expansive, and so ambiguous that in the end we come to ask ourselves: Hey, wait a minute. Did we ever get to define the soul? What happened to the itch we seemed to neatly avoid scratching? Spirituality is one thing, but does it necessarily zero in on the soul? *Maybe we have souls even if we do not choose to be spiritual?*

Even the bold, revolutionary ideas of James Hillman, who embraces the concept of soul in psychology, seem to stop short of a definitive understanding of the soul. In his work, *Revisioning Psychology*, he does just that, revising the definition of psychology to incorporate the soul, almost like bringing it back to where it started before it digressed. Inspired by Carl Jung, Hillman does introduce the concept of "soul searching" in order to understand the big picture and he does move psychology from its strict reductionist approach to a more abstract, imaginative approach. But

---

[2] *The Battle of Behaviorism: An Exposition and an Exposure*, (New York: W.W. Norton & Co., 1929), 13.

[3] *The Soul of Psychotherapy: Recapturing the Spiritual Dimension in the Therapeutic Encounter*, (New York: The Free Press, 1998), 4.

[4] *Psychotherapy and Spirit*, (Albany: State University of New York Press, 1997), 8.

when it comes to actually defining the soul he uses poetry and metaphor, almost dancing around it because, as he says, he can never grasp it:

> It is as if consciousness rests upon a self-sustaining and imaginative substrate—an inner place or deeper person or ongoing presence – that is simply there even when all our subjectivity, ego and consciousness go into eclipse. Soul appears as a factor independent of the events in which we are immersed. Though I cannot identify soul with anything else, I also can never grasp it apart from other things, perhaps because it is like a reflection in a flowing mirror, or like the moon which mediates only borrowed light.[5]

This is very beautiful and elegant prose and seems headed in the right direction, but as I said before – are we missing something here?

What if we are not expected to thrash around in the murky waters of human speculation in search of a definition, and are merely required to read up and learn about it? I realize that many people are wary of a theological approach, but should they be so wary that they will not even read what there is about the subject? It takes a good deal of conviction to adamantly refuse such an opportunity. Ironically, some people are even religious in their stance against religion. As I mentioned in the first chapter, this book aims to present the information, details that you may never have heard of before. Let us touch on some of the concepts of the soul from a Torah point of view.

There are actually two main types of souls inherent in a human being. The first is the animal soul that is common to all living creatures; the second is the Divine Soul that is unique to human beings alone. The animal soul is called the *Nefesh*; the Divine Soul is called the *Neshamah*.

The *Nefesh*

The *Nefesh*, the life force of the body, sustains it and enables it to function in the world. The instinctual drive to live, triggering necessary physiological responses, is thus called the animal soul since it is no different than the living forces present in animals. A human's *Nefesh*, however, is more advanced in terms of function and capability. A human's capacity for imagination, intelligence, and memory distinguishes him or her from other creatures. Yet, even if they appear to extend beyond it, these advanced capabilities are still a part of the human's animal side.

The *Neshamah*

The *Neshamah* is an additional soul placed in people to give them the opportunity to connect with their spiritual roots. Suddenly the human is a dynamic entity in which the opportunity exists for spiritual advancement. Without this soul, it would be impossible to advance spiritually. Other creatures do not have this soul and thus do not have the opportunity to advance spiritually. In the

---

[5] *Revisioning Psychology*, (New York: Harper & Row, 1975), x.

process of creating the first human being, the Torah tells us that God "blew into [man's] nostrils the *Neshamah* of life." This is the "breath" that distinguishes us from other creatures.[6] The *Neshamah* yearns for spiritual fulfillment, achieved through the human's unique challenge of making the right choices in life.

How do we explain this challenge? The *Neshamah* and the *Nefesh* reside in the same body.[7] By the very nature of their definitions, I am sure you will realize that the *Nefesh* and the *Neshamah* are opposites from each other. The *Neshamah* yearns for spiritual fulfillment; the *Nefesh* aches for instinctual fulfillment. Quite often a person can actually sense these two souls being at odds with each other. What is good for you instinctually is not necessarily good for you spiritually. Even a gut feeling may seem right to you, but from the *Neshamah*'s point of view it could be bad for you. Hence, a human experiences inner conflict. This may occur not only once or twice but a number of times daily. Someone cuts you off in traffic. One part of you directs you to react quickly out of anger and instinctual defensiveness; another part tells you not to descend to that level. The last slice of your fourth serving of pizza awaits you. You're full anyway. But you just can't let it go…. Or another conflict—a box-office hit is showing right now but you have that boring meeting to go to…. There are enough of these daily battles to make you overly self-conscious, causing you to suspect that you are afflicted with a dual personality.

But don't worry, you're normal. It is specifically in the heat of these ordinary, everyday confrontations where the human's potential for spiritual growth is realized. Not necessarily through meditation, not through levitation, but through action.[8] As you choose to let the *Neshamah* win the battle, you inch yourself closer to spiritual fulfillment. Remember we said that the human being has a microcosm of God's capacity to create? When we make the right choices, when we are creating, that's when our power as human beings is most keenly expressed. These seemingly mundane tests are the vital tools to growth. That is the whole reason why they're there. Animals do not have these tests. If you beg to differ, I encourage you to find me a cheetah who stops in his tracks while chasing a deer, thinking, "Well, maybe I shouldn't—I mean, the poor deer does look frightened…." Cheetahs do not suffer moral dilemmas.

---

[6] The Hebrew word for breath is *neshimah* which actually shares the same grammatical root as the word, *neshama*

[7] There is actually a third type of soul, called the *ruach* lit. wind, that interplays with these two souls. A fascinating description of the interrelation of these souls is found in the notes to the classic philosophical work, *Derech Hashem*, *The Way Of God*, by Rabbi Moshe Chaim Luzzato (1707–1746). In the notes, Rabbi Yosef Begun likens the interaction of the souls to the process of blowing glass. In glassblowing, the breath (likened to the Neshamah) of the glass blower, flows as a wind (*ruach*) through the glassblowing pipe, and finally comes to rest in the vessel that is being formed. (The root of the word Nefesh" is rest). Thus all that is noticeable to us is the Nefesh because it is the "condensed" part. From *The Way of God*, Feldheim Publishers, Sixth Edition, 1997

[8] The Torah does have an approach to meditation, but it must be understood in context of certain Torah principles. See *Jewish Meditation: A Practical Guide*, by Rabbi Aryeh Kaplan

It is important that you note these two terms, the *Nefesh* and the *Neshamah*. Since they have starring roles in nearly all aspects of our lives, they will have starring roles in nearly all aspects of this book. You will see how the tension and friction between them manifest themselves differently for every type of challenge. You will see how they are represented in the realm of order and fitness, in the realm of anger, of speech, of giving, of goal setting, and of happiness. They are always at work and never retire. Their interrelationship is at the core of our growth.

It is fascinating to discover that the real potential for spiritual growth is right under our noses. The path to spiritual fulfillment neither costs money nor requires fancy excursions anywhere. Why do we tend to think the secret lies elsewhere? Because we don't want to work hard. We really don't. Just to avoid ourselves, we design grandiose spiritual "isms" that we passionately embrace. What a shame. Inner conflict is a gift God gave us. It is an honor and a privilege to be able to face the challenge. There is so much potential here, and yet we slither past it believing that utopia is a place free of conflict.

Free of conflict? How will you grow spiritually? You'll be stuck on a plateau. Lying flat on a beach chair (with the coconuts dropping harmlessly around you) is instinctually a very appealing picture. Some people actually work their whole lives in the hope of reaching just this point. Yet the pamphlet that contains the picture all-too-often ends up being more enticing than the experience itself![9] This is because existence is almost futile without the opportunity for growth; and, even though difficult to admit it, the human being often senses as much. Genuine spiritual growth comes from winning the challenge, not by avoiding it all together. This is what (in the first chapter) we termed "the right kind of creativity"—being bold enough to stare at our inner selves and to resolve to make the right choices.

However, what we are speaking about now is the ideal. The ideal is that the conflict is there, that it's clearly defined, and that the correct path is just as clear. Most of us are so clouded by images and bombarded by ideologies, both subtle and overt, that we are 'layered' by excesses. We cannot see through to recognize and delineate the conflicts, let alone the resolutions. This is why we need to go on the *Soul Diet*. We need to remove all the obstacles, clean the slate of all the junk so that we can take a good look at ourselves. We need a few moments, days, or even weeks alone with our exposed core to determine where our conflicts lie. Once we've achieved that level of clarity we can build again, not by getting rid of the conflicts but having clarity on the right choices. Gaining this clarity is the emphasis, because, as noted, there is no happiness like the resolution of doubt.

Let's begin step one.

---

[9] This concept is discussed further in Chapter 13, *The Happy Factor*.

4

Step 1: The Media Fast

YES, THERE ARE MANY OF US WHO BEMOAN the giant grip the media has on our society. We roll our eyes at its sensationalism, we are enraged by its partiality, and we are annoyed by its invasion of privacy. Yet, for the most part, we treat the media like a spouse—the spouse with all those annoying habits: the spouse who has the audacity to come home late without calling; the spouse who never bothers to clean up; the spouse who buys things he or she cannot afford. But when it comes down to it, we love our spouses and wouldn't trade them for anyone else. With all the media's faults, it has been consecrated as the world's spouse for life. The divorce rate is very low, almost non-existent. Very few people think of separating from the media, and even fewer actually go through with it.

Occasionally I get a telemarketing call from a major newspaper trying to sell me a subscription. When I reply that I don't read newspapers, they are at a loss for words (quite a rare event, as you know). "You don't read newspapers at all?" they ask, after a while, deviating from their script. Some have even asked me why. Of course I cannot explain it to them in such a forum, but the point is that the shock evident in their reaction is quite revealing about how society views the media's permanent anchor in our everyday lives.

In this chapter, arguably the most difficult one of all, we are not going to divorce the media outright; rather, we are going to temporarily separate—to let the media go on its merry way for a period of two weeks so that we can take the first major step in clearing the clutter from our lives.

What's the Big Deal?

OK, since you involuntarily asked this question, I am going to detail my response according to each of the mediums that present a problem, beginning with television.

TV or Not TV – Is There Really a Question?

As for the content of television, it is not a secret that undesirable material is rampant on many stations and channels. For many years complaints have been voiced against the violence and explicit material aired to the public, and about its detrimental effects, especially for children. In comparison to those who do not watch, well-documented research substantiates claims of increased violent behavior and deterioration in moral standards among avid viewers. Although this is a serious problem, my focus is not so much on television content as on the more subtle, detrimental effects that receive less attention from lobbyists and consumer advocates.

In "What they don't want you to know about television and videos,"[1] Rabbi Lawrence Kelemen refers to the "commercialism" of television where he remarks that "television does not exist to entertain us; it exists to sell to us." He quotes Dr. John Condry, a professor of human development and family studies at Cornell University who wrote that, "the task of those who program television is to capture the public's attention and to hold it long enough to advertise a product."[2]

According to this, it seems that the commercials should not be regarded as the intervals between programming—rather the programming should be regarded as the intervals between commercials. What this means is that a viewer willingly subjects him or her self to hours of a presentation that in its essence is a sales pitch. As Kelemen puts it, "commercials are intended to create a feeling of lack in the viewer, a deep ache that can only be assuaged by purchasing the product."[3]

That a little box in your living room can convince you that your life is lacking should not be a surprise. Dazzling film and computer technology ensures that the right nerve buttons in our brains and our egos are pressed so that we digest the new information, incorporating it almost immediately into our identity. Needs are invented where none existed beforehand. This is not mere clutter. This can be quite disorienting. You can suddenly find yourself in a place you never intended to be, like someone has switched the point on the railroad tracks while you weren't looking. Professor Erik Barnouw, radio and television pioneer, had this to say: "The creators of advertising can claim that no one takes it all very seriously; it is all more or less in fun. The viewer's self-respect requires rejection of most commercials on the conscious level, along with some ridicule. Beneath the ridicule the commercial does its work."[4]

If we are to follow the premise of this book, we have to give those nerve buttons a break or else we will be taking direction from the box in the living room and not from the head on our shoulders. We have to consider clicking off the sales pitch, for a while at least. Another problem that deserves our attention is that television shots are fired rapidly, changing very frequently, so that the eye takes in multiple images every minute. Aside from the bombardment of images creating a tremendous amount of clutter (and you know what I have to say about that) it can have the effect of training the mind to pay attention only for short bursts, since each screen change is a stimulus that takes the burden off our power of concentration. As Keleman quotes Robert MacNeil, the "idea is to keep everything brief, not to strain the attention of anyone but instead to provide constant stimulation through variety, novelty, action and movement."[5]

---

[1] Abridged from the "Television" Chapter in *To Kindle a Soul*. (Michigan: Targum/Feldheim, 2002), 19.

[2] ibid., 20.

[3] ibid.

[4] *The Sponsor: Notes on a Modern Potentate*. (New York: Oxford University Press, 1978), 83.

[5] Kelemen, 28.

It could possibly help explain the experiences I have had in teaching children who, not through ill-intention, behave in the class as though someone has injected them with rocket fuel. These are sweet, innocent children who, while I am teaching, jump up from their desks for no apparent reason, swing their arms and legs in countless different directions and generally cannot sit still for longer than a couple of seconds. Why? Because my screen doesn't change. After a few seconds *I am still there*! How do we expect anyone who is subjected to this TV imagery invasion to grow up with a steady, unwavering focus that will steer him or her through life with clarity? Clarity is almost impossible while this over-stimulation is at work for hours on end every single day.

The most subtle effect of all is also, I believe, the most subversive. On the surface this effect appears innocuous. Actually people are so taken by it that they embrace it as a celebration of art and expression. But they are generally unaware of its power to gradually infiltrate our thought systems so that, after a while, we begin to think differently. To what am I referring? To the confusion of reality and fantasy.

As Seen on TV.

Consider the following: the two wine goblets are filled to the brim and shimmer in the moonlight on the deck of the ship. Charley leans over the table for two and tells his wife, "Vera, these have been the best twenty-five years of my life."

Tears collect in the corners of Vera's eyes and she smiles at him, her hair perfectly combed so that it drapes gently like a curtain over her evening dress that sparkles along with the wine. Invisible violins serenade the two of them, fading just long enough for the waiter to deposit their *hors d'oeuvres*. Then the music becomes too loud for you to hear their conversation, though you do see them laughing with abandon about something Vera has said, and the tempo and the pitch of the violins reflect their sheer joy of this moment etched in time….

"Ma'am," the usher whispers to you.

Startled, you look up. "Yes?"

"Do you have a white Toyota?"

"Yes." You're missing the anniversary diamond Charley is unveiling.

"Your lights are on."

"Thank you," you say politely, although the mumbling under your breath has already begun in earnest. You clamber out of the cinema, your eyes straining against the bright mall lights. The music has gone. The moonlight has gone. Vera and Charley have gone and by the time you get to your car you might have to find someone to help you jumpstart it. As you walk out into the drizzle, you're trying to remind yourself where you left the jumper cables the last time this happened….

Back home, Norman walks through the door as you're microwaving a TV dinner. He is holding a handkerchief to his nose because of all the pollen in the air. You want to greet him properly, but the phone rings and it's your daughter who has missed her ride back from the skating rink downtown, and could somebody pick her up? Just before you go to sleep that night your mind drifts to Vera and Charley; and the disappointment settles in, not so much that you were interrupted and had to jumpstart your car but that your life misses something that Vera and Charley have. It gives you a dull ache that you imagine would be assuaged by striving more and more to be like Vera and Charley. So the next day you buy (with a red face because Norman has asked you to cut down on spending) a jacket for Norman that Charley would wear. You also try on a number of different dresses you will buy in the future once you will get down to Vera's weight. That is why, by the way, this morning you strengthened your resolve not to put sugar in your coffee, and to stay far away from carbohydrates. Later that evening you present the jacket to Norman, trying to capture the ambience of the moonlit ship deck floating in your mind. Norman's first response is akin to a slot machine reeling with the numbers of their joint checking account at Washington Mutual. Needless to say, he has no idea that he has to behave like Charley.

Consider the next scenario: With a wry smile and a practiced stare, Michael Besario LLM, addresses the men and women of the jury. His words pound at their conscience like a hammer, splintering their resistance with exquisite articulation and reasoning. The closing argument draws gasps just at the right moment. The background music reaches a crescendo and he retreats to a thunderous silence. This scene is one of many that has sold you lock stock and barrel on taking up law as a career. Right now, you're still stuck in your undergraduate degree in anthropology, but don't tell anyone that you've visited a particular furniture store several times where you've stood behind a mahogany desk and silently assumed the role of Michael Besario. Years down the line when you actually do become a clerk and get loaded with a mountain of paperwork, you cannot understand why the music isn't playing, why the movies never showed the sheer volume of monotonous jargon and bureaucracy awaiting you every morning.

Meanwhile you're the kid mesmerized by power-packed action adventure films where laser beams and foul language meet to conquer the world. Your mommy suddenly clicks it off because you have English grammar homework to do. Need I elaborate? What is happening in this disturbing process is a reversal of the normative function of entertainment. Rather than drawing on the values observed in society and adapting them for the purpose of dramatization, society has begun to draw on the values observed in entertainment and to adopt them as a culture.

As part of a broader study in the Cook Islands, the impact on locals of western commercials broadcast to them was observed and analyzed.

> Following a series of Coca Cola commercials, for example, demand for Coke expanded dramatically. What was most interesting about the boom in sales was that purchasers began demanding Coke in bottles, like the ones they saw on television.[6]

---

[6] Duane Varan, "The Cultural Erosion Metaphor and the Transcultural Impact of Media Systems," *Journal of Communication*, Spring 1998. 48.2: 58.

If media can shape the bottles from which we insist on drinking, it can also shape the directives by which we insist on living our lives. As Richard W. Pollay writes, "Commercial persuasion appears to program not only our shopping and product use behavior but also the larger domain of our social roles, language, goals, values, and the sources of meaning in our culture."[7]

In fact, according to Neil Postman, television does not merely shape our culture, it has "gradually *become* our culture."[8] This is true even though the values espoused are based purely in fantasy and often have no substance to them whatsoever. As Postman comments, "We all build castles in the air. The problems come when we try to *live* in them."[9] This is particularly the case when the theme is underdog-succeeding-to-become-champion, and in these films the underdog *always* succeeds in becoming champion, generating a whole subculture of "I can do it" disciples taking leaps where they should not necessarily be leaping. Remember, the head should drive the heart. There is room for positive thinking, but the hype of "Don't let anyone stop you from reaching your goal" is not the magical cure it's touted to be and is often based on spontaneous emotion devoid of sound reasoning.

This is why I regard this problem as the most subversive. The problem of violence and immorality on television has long been under fire, but the subtleties I am referring to here receive scant attention. They can surreptitiously take people away from what is real and what is objectively good for them, all the while finding favor in the eye of the public as invaluable contributions to artistic thought and expression. If we'd give it a little thought, we'd realize just how pervasive this concept is in Western consciousness. Value systems, dreams and aspirations so often stem from a Hollywood source. All a famous actress need do is wear something strikingly different and an entire mode of dress is spawned that would never have existed if it weren't for her. All a famous producer need do is select a particular period in history as the setting for a mega-thriller, and a whole population of students emerge eager to digest information about that era that would otherwise never have interested them

Where would Western interest in Chinese Martial Arts be without Bruce Lee? Would people have altered their cars for super performance if it weren't for the film, *The Fast and the Furious?* Would there ever have been a disco craze without *Saturday Night Live?* And how many role models and icons held dear by society *do not* come from Hollywood? There would be a gaping hole in modern culture were it not for its influence. At first glance, you may be asking: well, what's wrong with that? If Hollywood is inspiring devotees to history and culture, then it's a good thing, isn't it?

---

[7] Curator, History of Advertising Archives, University of British Columbia, in "The Distorted Mirror: Reflections on the Unintended Consequences of Advertising," *Journal of Marketing*, Vol. 50, April 1986: 21.

[8] *Amusing Ourselves to Death, Public Discourse in the Age of Show Business*, (New York: Penguin Books, 1985), 79.

[9] Ibid., 77.

I am not implying whether it's necessarily good or bad. I'm merely pointing out the extent to which our culture is shaped by the silver screen. Does that not have implications for what our lives would be like if they were free of that influence? In other words, are we not subtly entering the realm of indoctrination here? Yes, indoctrination can sometimes be good; but it is, after all, indoctrination. Is that not at least worth exploring? That's why this book suggests removing all this stimulation we get from television and film for a period of time so that we may regain a fresh, untainted perspective on ourselves.

Newspapers and Other Print Media

OK. So what could be the problem here? you ask. Surely there is nothing wrong with reading. All the proponents of culture preservation are trying to get more people to read. There are no moving images slipping and sliding across your vision to send you into a trance. You are actively involved in deciphering the material in front of you; it encourages cognitive development and stimulation of the imagination etc.… Yes, exactly. You become actively involved in every single incident that hits the planet from Fiji to Finland, from Vermont to Vladivostok, from who's playing Wimbledon to who has the West Nile Virus – all in one neat little package spread out in front of you. A global sandwich with everything on it for you to digest in one sitting. Imagine for a moment how much clutter we are taking in merely by opening one page of a newspaper – talk about spiritual calories!

"But how will I know what's going on in the world if you won't even let me read newspapers?" you ask, exasperated. Let's dissect that question. What you are asking can be understood in two ways:

A. I *need* to know what is going on because it might apply to me and require some sort of response on my part, for example a terrorist warning, God forbid; or I need to know because if there is tragedy on the other side of the world in which I can do my part to help, through monetary contributions, political lobbying or even plain empathy for other people's situations. Or I need to know what the weather forecast is so that I can plan my day accordingly. Or I need to get the stock reports. These are all valid practical motivations for being in touch with the news.

B. I *want* to know what is going on because it is very interesting, gives me broader exposure to the outside world, makes me a worldly person. And, to be honest, I like the drama of a corporate fraud investigation or a political cover up. I'm hooked on a particular murder trial that is unfolding like a Scott Turow novel. I'm intrigued by intelligence failures the likes of which Tom Clancy couldn't dream up.

You guessed that I am not particularly enamored of motivation B. Being worldly today constitutes a willingness to be inundated with a myriad of details and emotions that somehow find space in our heads. All the world's issues, even the most trivial in nature, blend with everything else in a mesh of images and facts that seek entry into our conscience. Those tabloids and magazines that adorn the check-out counter at the local store are expertly designed to quench one's thirst for juicy trivia. Henry David Thoreau[10] foresaw this phenomenon with the invention of the telegraph. "We are eager to tunnel under the Atlantic and bring the old world some weeks nearer to the new; but perchance the first news that will leak through into the broad flapping American ear will be that Princess Adelaide has the whooping cough."[11]

As for the claim that the more you pack in the more clarity you have, it's difficult to believe. Clarity can only come from unadulterated focus, not from a collage of images and ideas that collect in your head. Genuine worldliness comes from an intelligently focused perspective on where you stand in the world and where your limits are. If your reason for reading print media is Motivation A, every effort should be spent in obtaining a summary bulletin of the headline news, customized with the specifics you need. It is easy to get this electronically, but, for reasons expounded on later, it is preferable to get it in hard copy. Because print media lacks the capacity to stimulate through audio visual means, the commercials are less overpowering than those appearing on television. Not only does the image remain still, but, since there are other options laid out on the page to capture one's interest, the eye does not necessarily travel directly to the commercial. Nevertheless, it is worth commenting on what advertisers have done to address this "weakness" in potency:

Catch the Eye or Die

You open the paper or a magazine and the following words greet you: "The Pinnacle. Be there." The words are colored silver like a sword cutting through the large black background. Apart from a tiny symbol on the bottom, there is nothing else on this half-page advertisement. What is being advertised here? A music concert called "The Pinnacle"? A goal-setting course, helping you to reach "The Pinnacle"? A vacation spot called "The Pinnacle"?

No, no, no. It's for a car, of course.

"A car?" you stammer. Yes, a luxury car, because when you buy this car you have reached the pinnacle. You really don't need to know anything about the car itself. And there will be many, many people who will walk into a dealership, if not now, later, and test drive the car, lamely peppering the salesperson with a question here and there about the actual car, but in the back of their minds they are there to reach the pinnacle. It's difficult to imagine that such an advertisement receives much ridicule; otherwise the company would not be spending so much money on it. This means that illusion and fantasy have been comfortably welcomed into reality, where the variables of psychological motivation in product purchases take center stage and drown out the physical product itself.

As Neil Postman writes, "The distance between rationality and advertising is now so wide that it is difficult to remember that there once existed a connection between them."[12] Thus, even

---

[10] Quoted by Postman in *Amusing Ourselves to Death,* 65.

[11] *Walden,* (Boston: Houghton-Mifflin, 1957), 36.

[12] Ibid., 128.

though print media lacks the audio visual advantages of other media it still succeeds in perpetuating a world of illusion, in helping to erase the line between fantasy and reality, in guiding people along a path that exists only in a netherworld, like a twilight zone, where people buy cars because they want to reach the pinnacle.

As if I needed to remind you, living in the twilight zone is a no-no.

The slogan-oriented trend—trying to crunch the essence of a multi-dimensional item into a tiny capsule of flashy rhetoric—is also symptomatic of a deeper, more complex societal problem that is best illustrated when discussing talk-show radio.[13]

Small Talk

A medium of expression that is becoming increasingly popular is the talk show concept where, basically, not only does the radio talk to you but also you can actually talk to the radio. This is a live "letters to the editor" that encourages your input and enables interactive discussion, capturing your feelings and passion in raw, undiluted form. And people like it. They like to hear other people's blood boiling. They also enjoy having their own blood boiling because the rush of adrenaline is like mental and verbal bungee-jumping. Suddenly you're alive, your opinions flying across the airwaves and knocking the wind out of some other opinion.

Ronnie from Reno and Nuclear Energy

Ronnie is livid. He is adjusting the strap of his wristwatch and listening to a debate on the dangers posed by nuclear reactors and their waste—something about the government's plan to bury it at Yucca Mountain in Nevada by 2010. All he knows is that the concept of nuclear power gets his goat. Several years ago, he saw *The Day After* and he hasn't been able to live those images down. He is infuriated by people's obsession with big toys such as missiles and atomic bombs at the expense of innocent lives. So he calls in. After only his second try, he gets through. His elation is tempered only by his convictions.

"Let's go to Ronnie from Reno. Ronnie, what can I do for you?"

"Hi, John," Ronnie stammers, holding back his indignation. "I just wanted to say that I believe this whole idea of nuclear power is a veiled attempt to control others. With weapons of mass destruction a country can feel all powerful, as though it has a sword to brandish if someone threatens them. It's almost medieval and archaic. Psychologically—"

---

[13] I am the first to admit my guilt in creating a title and concept called "The Soul Diet" and using other such sub-titles which hardly do justice to a serious, vastly complex subject. Ideally this would be a much larger scholarly work, probably entitled "A systemized program to establish clear healthy directives through elimination of environmental over-stimulation." Unfortunately I cannot start off speaking a language that runs against the contemporary style if I want to attract public attention to my message. My hope is that once I have obtained your interest, we can shift to a less audacious, more comprehensive style.

"Ronnie," John interrupts.

But he won't let John stop him until he's finished his point. "It's a magnification of the ego unleashed, and it's dressed up so well with…."

"One second, Ronnie," John says, more forcefully. "We're not talking about a nuclear weapons program here. We're talking about nuclear power plants that use nuclear energy to create electric power."

John is not a maven on nuclear energy, but in preparing for the show he did a little research to cover the basics. He may not be clear on the intricacies of nuclear fission, alpha and beta particles and gamma rays, but he knows enough to understand that nuclear weapons are not produced at a nuclear power plant. Ronnie is thunderstruck for a split second. But there is no way on earth he would let half a million listeners be spectator to his embarrassment. "I know that," he swallows. "But it's all the same thing when it comes down to it. Nuclear energy is nuclear energy, and harnessing one medium will eventually lead to harnessing another." Ronnie is relieved to find that John does not refute his argument. But it's hard to tell what John thinks because he has already moved on to the next caller.

Rosalie has never seen a nuclear reactor before. Her major in college was Contemporary Philosophy, and she stayed away from the sciences because "it just wasn't me." Yet, she is not considered out of line for taking a public stand in an area she knows nothing about. In fact she is actually invited to share her views and shed some "light" on the subject.

And light it is, as light as a feather, since conventional wisdom does not have to be wholly substantive. As peripheral as your argument may be, as long as what you have to say is appealing you will win over others. This is where the talk show principle shares common ground with the "slogan concept" of print media mentioned earlier: you don't have to know the facts. You just have to like the jingle.

In "Vox Populi as Cable Programming Strategy," Jeffrey P. Jones elaborates. "The talk show mingles the "professional" or "expert" with the "amateur," the guest or participant who appears by virtue of particular personal experience or simple audience membership. It shrewdly combines the folk and the popular with the mass, the immediate and the interpersonal with the mediated…. This circularity and undecidability are as characteristic of the talk show as the very name itself. Is it "talk" or "show"? Conversation or spectacle?"

Jones comments that rapid technological advancement and the advent of the "global village" has facilitated a narrowing of the gap between professionals and amateurs so that people are able to express their dissatisfaction more easily and frequently. "Problems associated with recalcitrant politicians and bureaucracies would disappear, the rhetoric seemed to suggest, as people became empowered by new communication technologies to participate in decisions that govern their lives." [14]

---

[14] *Journal of Popular Film and Television*, Spring 2003, 31.1: 18.

But this empowerment, as we have observed, does not necessarily have any substance to it. Many people enjoy the sensation of having that power even if it is based on ignorance, and thus they play into the hands of the marketers who are less interested in their opinions than they are in the popularity of the show. If this is what brings in the money, then this is what is going to be presented. You know that feeling when a salesperson comes over to you and asks you, "How are you doing today?" Yes, he is interested in your answer; not for the answer, but for the sale that's pending on your positive reaction.

An additional, more recognized problem is the partiality of a talk show. It is rare to find a show that is non-partisan, has no agenda whether subtle or overt, and is bold enough to present a balanced viewpoint on an issue. Such a show would probably sound like a nature documentary and promptly put the adrenaline-crazed listener to sleep. That, I'm afraid, does not bring in the money.

Where does this leave us? Tuning into talk show radio adds to your clutter by swamping you with issues that are generally not methodically and fairly substantiated; it hooks you to its loud pulsating rhythm and, once again, lures you along the intersection of fantasy and reality so that an accurate, balanced perspective on your life is utterly boring and doesn't do anything for you. It requires a kind of rehabilitation process so that we can be resensitized to the issues that are real, the issues to which we have been numbed because they lack the immediate potency of a talk show discussion.

One medium in particular distinguishes itself by exhibiting the worst properties of all the other mediums presented thus far. If you thought I've been a touch negative so far, wait until you read what's coming next. Before I do go there, let me address this very comment. I am not a negative person by nature. I'm not always out to see the faults in everything. Believe it or not, I am paving the way to a positivism that is real, that is solid, that is not ethereal or transitory but that will become an integral part of you rather than a flight of fancy. In order to do that, we need to do some cleaning up. I know this sounds like an extreme diet. However, its aim is not to starve you to death, but to starve you to life!

Beauty and the Beast

There are many advantages to the Internet. In a commercial world where real estate has become scarce, the advent of limitless cyberspace has fueled business and economy (even with burst bubbles), has opened up worlds of previously inaccessible information to the average person at the click of a button and has provided lightning-quick alternatives to standard forms of communication and interaction, to the point that the Internet has revolutionized everyday living. This we all know.

We also know that this beauty can turn into the beast. First, the easy accessibility of unsuitable material is an obvious problem. Whether or not government should get involved in protecting the public from this ease of access has been brought up in the courts, but this is not what I intend to focus on. Again it's the subtleties not receiving much attention that need to be examined.

The Wall Street Journal reported several observations concerning the effect of the Internet on children. It points out that although children learn the skills necessary for internet and computer usage much quicker than do adults, "children who grow up with the Internet as an accepted part of their lives face other challenges. Specifically, many experts doubt that emotional development can keep pace with the neurological changes brought about by early and persistent exposure to computers and multimedia imagery. There is, after all, a large difference between knowing something intellectually and understanding it emotionally."[15]

Repeating a theme we have mentioned with other digital media, the article also quotes Leon Hoffman, a New York-based child psychoanalyst who remarks that, "sorting out what's real" often proves difficult for kids, and that "children don't realize when it's fake."[16]

This study brings to mind something else worth noting here. There is a common tendency to perceive the problems associated with the media's influence, particularly the Internet, as pertinent only to children. We feel compelled to protect our kids and somehow think that we adults are immune. Alternatively, we imagine that adults have lost that special innocence anyway, and so it seems there's nothing left to protect. We've been tainted already, so what difference would it make to taint us further?

However you look at it, this notion of non-applicability is a fallacy. Turning a certain age does not grant us a license to slacken and succumb to all the lures that pulse around us. For many, becoming an adult means becoming exempt from discipline as though we have "served our time" as a child and now its time to "have fun." Children are suffering through basic training, and the adults are sitting in the officers' lounge.

Even if your concern is only for yourself and not for your child, bear in mind that the best training children can get is to witness discipline in their parents. Children learn best by osmosis, the unspoken principles exhibited by their parents' behavior, the way their parents speak, the way they conduct themselves under pressure, how focused they are, how they control themselves, how closely they stick to their goals. Children who are expected to behave in a focused, dignified manner will be confused, at best, by their parents' unfocused, undignified manner.

But wait, you object. You can't lump kids and adults into the same category. Adults know how to handle the Internet, sort through the jumble, control themselves, temper the invasion, filter the information, employ common sense and…. Yeah. Sure!

Newsweek reveals to just what extent the Internet contributes to a startling phenomenon: women in established, mostly secure marriages engaging in infidelity.[17] It relates the experience of John LaSage who finds his wife of twenty-four years had disappeared without a trace. The computer he had bought her four months previously turned out to be the focus of the investigation. His wife

---

[15] Yochi J. Dreazen and Rachel Emma Silverman, "Raised in Cyberspace: Using Computers can quickly become second nature to children; that isn't necessarily such a good thing," *The Wall Street Journal Millennium (A Special Report): Politics & Society*. Dec 31, 1999: R.47.

[16] Ibid.

[17] Lorraine Ali and Lisa Miller, "The Secret Lives of Wives," *Newsweek*. July 12, 2004: 47.

had stayed up until 3 or 4 a.m., browsing online. She had told him she was doing research for a romance novel she was writing. Instead she had set up a chat room.

"I can't tell you how excruciating it was to read the e-mails from people supposedly speaking with my wife, but she wasn't talking like my wife. That was just weird."[18] Of course, this phenomenon is not limited to women being unfaithful, and it certainly happens the other way around too. But, in a sad way, the concept of a man's unfaithfulness to his wife does not shock anymore. What makes this story newsworthy is the reversal of the perception of a married woman's general sensibilities and her groundedness, the sense that she would never do anything so utterly foolish as to destroy her marriage just like that.

The article does list other contributing factors, but the real bombshells are dropped in discussing the role of the Internet, specifically the idea that some women fancy starting a web site for married women who want to date. It seems that this attitude, together with John's observations about his wife that "she wasn't talking like my wife," can help us understand the nature of the Internet's influence: There is almost an Orwellian quality to the Internet's pervasiveness. It is certainly eerie that it can take ordinary rational beings and inflate them with ideas that are limited only by the outer edges of cyberspace. Possibilities are endless, now that the global village is at our fingertips, and if fantasy and reality were ever confused, the Internet has made this its trademark. People are acting out their fantasies not necessarily because they enjoy indulging in what is taboo, but because there is no such thing as fantasy anymore. *Everything* is real. Your fantasy is just as real as the coffee mug next to your keyboard.

Greg Parmeter, editorialist for Northern State University's online magazine, *The Exponent*, comments as follows: "Dinner conversation at the family table is virtually non-existent anymore. The 'real' conversations are on the discussion boards discussing everything from world politics to the next Star Wars movie. So here's the question: between the Web and the world, what's really 'real'?"[19]

It is no wonder that John's wife wasn't talking like herself, because "herself" had been redefined by her voyages into cyberspace. Once the rules have permitted an overlap of fantasy and reality, it is hard to label anything as outlandish. In fact the only thing that would be considered outlandish is a movement to drastically curb the Internet's presence in our lives. It is only a decade or so in operation but it has become as indispensable as the shirts on our backs.

If this does not convince you to embark on an Internet fast, and you're thinking, "Well, I'm much more of a moderate person, I don't react so impulsively," then consider the problem we first encountered when discussing talk shows and slogan-oriented presentations. The tendency to barely scratch the surface of an issue and yet be considered knowledgeable and insightful is not unrelated to the effects of the Internet. That harmless little mouse that scurries across its mat enables you

[18] Ibid.

[19] "Losing Touch in the Cyber-Age," *The Exponent*. 2002.

to click here and click there for instant access, instant feedback, and instant understanding of complex subjects. An instant understanding of a complex subject is a paradox. It does not do justice to an intricate, involved subject by demanding it be condensed into a sentence or two. And I say "demand" because web surfers would generally not be able to tolerate a comprehensive thirty page treatise presented as a response to their click button. Imagine a box appearing across your computer screen saying, "I'm sorry, but the information you have requested will actually require you to purchase two textbooks and attend a course." What is likely to happen is that the surfer will hit the "back" button and select a different option. Thus we see how the Internet compounds the problem of instant gratification, effectively dulling the sense of reverence people once had for true expertise. Anything that requires extensive research is avoided and deemed laborious, monotonous and even a waste of time.

In taking on the Media Fast, we hope to achieve a level of clarity that will enable us to re-embrace the virtues of genuine knowledge acquisition, speaking up about an issue only if one is qualified for it, if one has examined the need for it, and if one has considered its consequences. Hopefully we will be re-sensitized to those things we now consider dull, boring and a waste of time. We need to shut out the illusion of moonlit decks, the parody of Twilight Zone products, the passion of pop expertise, and the pseudo reality of cyberspace. We need to take that breath of metaphysical air.

Once we have emptied the cache we can build again, the right away. Once we have developed a healthy focus, it will equip us with strength and fortitude to steer through the multitude of images and messages coming our way.

In "The cultural erosion metaphor and the transcultural impact of media systems,"[20] Duane Varan employs the metaphor of soil erosion to illustrate the corrosive properties of the media; at the same time, he reveals which types of people will be more adversely affected than others. The idea is that just as soil erosion weakens and changes the constituency of the soil by exposing the lower layers to foreign elements, so, too, media systems weaken and change a culture by exposing it to foreign elements. However, the author points out that "where values are strongest, impact is least."[21] When values are firmly rooted and clearly defined, when healthy directives are established and maintained, then it will be possible to weather the media storm. But first, we need to clear the media slate.

So, What Exactly Do You Mean by a Media Fast?

Practically, this entails restricting your intake of media systems for a period of two weeks. In general you will not permit yourself to watch any television, go to movies, read newspapers or magazines, listen to talk-show radio and browse the Internet. The only exception, as outlined above is if you

---

[20] Ibid.

[21] Ibid.

absolutely need, and not want, to know information that only the media could provide for you. Obviously if you own an online business, you are not going to be able to take a hiatus from your entire operation for two weeks. But it behooves you to scrutinize your intentions. Be totally honest with yourself because it is only you who will lose out. If in the process of this introspection you find that you slightly suspect your motivations for staying connected, lean on the side of caution because your suspicions are probably correct. Even if you most definitely have to remain connected, restrict yourself to as limited an amount of time as possible with the medium. By the way, online bill pay is not an absolute need. It only became an absolute need when it was introduced to the public. You can (if you still remember how to lick a stamp) actually snail mail your payments and nobody will think any less of you. Remember, this severe abstinence is only for a period of two weeks, enough time for you to develop a greater focus and resolve.

Email

For those highly motivated Soul Dieters, you will register for an email-only system, (sans Internet), and it will be spam blocked and you will check your personal mail box only once (yes, just once) a day. Obviously, I cannot expect business people to follow the same guidelines, but again, this is the ideal model.

Otherwise, if you are not ready or able to drop the net then take the following precaution: when you go to check your mail, remain *standing*. Do not sit down at your chair by the computer, or better yet, remove the chair completely from your desk. Because once you sit down, it's like allowing yourself a little dessert, and one thing leads to another and before you know it you're checking out the latest scandal to hit Hollywood. If you own a laptop, avoid connecting to your server as much as possible. The truth is, unless you must use it for business, lock away the laptop! It's like carrying the global village with you wherever you go. Before you started reading this book, such a concept probably would have actually appealed to you. By now you may well realize how detrimental it is.

When to Begin the Fast

Now! Even before you finish this book. This diet is like any other in that it disdains procrastination. Don't wait until after the final episode of *The Sopranos* to begin your diet, just as you shouldn't wait until after the cheesecake party on Sunday to begin your diet.

Should I Do Each of These 10 Steps One at a Time?

You do not have to complete the media fast before beginning the next step (explained in the coming chapters[22]).

---

[22] See Models of Integration in Appendix I for a bigger picture of how to integrate all the steps of the Diet.

Withdrawal Symptoms

You may be laughing at this sub-heading. Does the diet concept really stretch that far? Well, it's for you to decide. Suddenly not spending hours in front of the television or the computer; getting into the car for your forty-five minute commute home and stopping yourself from turning on the talk-show; sitting on the couch without the grainy feel of a newspaper for your fingers to ruffle; wondering whether anything interesting has arrived in your e-mail box and not allowing yourself to check it…. All these situations will produce some level of frustration, as though you have an itch to scratch and can't reach it. It sounds an awful lot like withdrawal symptoms to me. These symptoms will make you aware just how much you have been dependent on these mediums for your daily dose. Suddenly not being involved with them could be disorienting, make you restless; and instead of giving you the peace of mind I am promising, it might make you irritable and unsatisfied. Don't worry. That's just part of the process. Anybody involved in rehabilitation will tell you that. It will take a while before you feel that urgency begin to dissipate, but eventually other notions and sensations will begin to occupy you. You will start to feel refreshed, alert, sensitized and calm. Above all, you will have a lot of time on your hands. But before I advise you on what to do with all this new-found time, we are going to create even more time in your schedule.

How is that possible? you ask. I'll tell you….

5

Step 2: Schedule Slimming

"Vanilla latte." The smoking cup of coffee is cheerfully announced, and a hand stretches to grab it. Other coffees follow suit, rhythmically deposited on a small, elegant pedestal, awaiting collection by the caffeine-hungry patrons who have just dropped over three dollars for their latest injection. It is not merely an injection of liquid that this coffee shop is peddling, but an injection of eclectic spirit transforming an ordinary drinking experience into one of artistic expression. The aroma of freshly brewed beverages joins with the vision of islands of people cradling their laptops and with the sound of soapy music wafting everywhere to produce a potpourri of creative cultural chemistry.

Sipping on their steaming caffeine fountains, seated in wide-bodied lounge chairs that look imported from Sunday afternoon porch chats, a particular group of patrons battle the noise and clutter around them to exchange words and wi-fi signals. What is their purpose here today? To while away the lazy afternoon hours with some friends? To bask in the summer sun as they study all the people who pass by? No. Actually, they're in the middle of a business meeting.

A *what?* You heard me. What better place to close a deal than an oasis of cultural revelry surrounded by honking horns, espresso and cappuccino vapors, and bubbly cell-phone chatter? This seems much better than sitting in a stuffy office that is dead quiet and where any attempt at injecting life into the air gets immediately quashed by the thick upholstery. They need the external stimuli. They need to *be somewhere*. Too much quiet would ruin the deal. It would also bore them, frustrate them, depress them, and even… scare them.

Scare them? What am I talking about? Well, I'm using a business meeting only as an example of how "the right place" ranks so high on our list of priorities. If we were to step back and observe how certain business gets conducted, we would be perplexed to see that noise is actually considered an attraction rather than a hindrance. Of course, the claim is that you have to get the prospective client in the right mood, entertain this individual, wine and dine and butter him or her up. A coffee shop is perfect for that. The noise is, in any case, something called White Noise that does not disturb your concentration.

But on closer inspection something else is going on here. (Here I go again.) There is an underlying gravitation toward noise, present not just in the business world. It seems to be a general trend in all spheres. If ever our lives begin to quiet down, we feel compelled to 'escape' the quiet to a place of stimulation. Even when people say they just wish they could have some quiet, very often it means they wish they could have some time on their own to relax with *some external stimulus* of their choice: book, video, computer, music. Just because there may be quiet, it does not mean there is no noise. Noise, for our purposes, means subjecting ourselves to a stimulus rather than spending time with our own thoughts. As noted in the previous chapter in discussing "Withdrawal Symptoms," we have become so accustomed to the barrage of external stimuli bombarding us that we begin to crave it when it is absent. Quiet is scary because it means we are alone with ourselves. You, the reader, who has been bold enough to read thus far, have shown interest in spending time really thinking about yourself, but it is not a very common phenomenon.

This notion of noise gravitation can help to explain why we pack our schedules to the limit with activities. We find ourselves continually booked with things to do. Some of those activities are necessary and some of them (if you are honest enough to admit it) are invented so that you can get your next dose of stimulation. Ask any family what their schedule is like and they are likely to answer, "tight." What with carpool, gym, community meetings, potlucks, art fairs, music festivals, hip-hop dancing practice, clarinet lessons, PTA functions, holiday carnivals, outdoor market days, air shows, vet appointments, family barbeques, warehouse closeouts, gift shopping, cocktail parties, fundraising dinners, do we have room to breathe? Have we left any room on that schedule for introspection? Not likely. This chapter aims at encouraging schedule slimming so that you will, indeed, free up some time to do more introspection.

There are more aspects to schedule jamming that run deeper than what we have already discussed.

Cocooning

This insightful term is extracted from an article by Sue Toye. She presents the findings of Glenn Stalker, a PhD student in sociology, that "time [Canadians] spent with friends and family at home dropped to 58 percent of their leisure time in 1998, a decrease of 5% from 1986. He also found that although people are spending slightly more time outside their home with friends and family in places like cafes and restaurants, this growth has not kept pace with the decline in home-centered social contact." To sum up this pattern, Toye notes that "People are cocooning more."[1] Schedule jamming contributes to this idea by creating individualized schedules that are mutually exclusive from other family members and intersect less and less often. To get everybody together at dinner time would require a merging of the schedules at the exact right time, kind of like hoping that all the factors come together for a lunar eclipse. This tendency toward cocooning can have the effect of detaching people from their close-knit core. Living in parallel universes even to those who are closest to you is another step toward jumbled, unhealthy thinking.

---

[1] *People Cocooning more, socializing less at home: study. Change in the use of the dwelling space result of social and demographic changes*, News@University of Toronto, Office of Web and Info Services, Division of University Advancement, University of Toronto, June 23, 2004.

Duty Free or Free of Duty?

Let's return to that business meeting in the coffee shop. A peek at the archives of all the meetings leading up to this meeting reveals a level of inefficiency that is both frustrating and perplexing. For some reason, conversation gets so easily diverted from the issue at hand that rarely is real progress made. One of the only concrete and verifiable hurdles jumped is a unanimous decision to hold *another* meeting to discuss things further. Yet none of the people in this group are keen on shining the spotlight on this level of inefficiency, because as long as it appears that things are moving, even if it's simply the decision to hold another meeting, the participants leave somewhat satisfied. There can be a game of illusion here in which many people are willing players, aided by the whirlwind of eclectic coffee culture spinning around them. And at the end of the day, not much is being done, really.

Not to mention that each participant has a daily schedule that reads like reams of HTML code. Meetings in Boston, conferences in Chicago, product presentations in L.A. With such full schedules, is there not a guarantee of progress and achievement? Is the fast track the only way to move in our world today? Would people rather be at home, working a 9 to 5 schedule that wouldn't wear them out so that they could spend more time with their families? Uh... sure.

> *I'd love to do that. The thing is that... it's really important to do what the workplace requires if you want to succeed. If this is the lifestyle the fast track demands, do I really have a choice?*

Only you can answer that question. If your heart is firmly in that direction, I cannot use rational argument to persuade you otherwise. We've discussed previously the hold the heart can have on the mind, and it's quite pointless to use mind-talk to speak to the heart. Even if it were true—that you cannot possibly alter your hectic schedule—there is still a palpable difference in attitude between one who embraces the fast track and one who deals with it, trying his best to navigate around it so that he can indeed spend more time with his family. The latter has internalized the fact that merely flying all over the place does not mean you are moving anywhere.

Do you recall the opening passage of this book when I referred immediately to a treadmill? I did not do so absent-mindedly. Really, much of today's perception of success, whether physical or spiritual, is analogous to the treadmill factor—running here, running there and not getting anywhere. The problem is compounded by commercialism that recognizes this inflated feeling people strive for, and proceeds to capitalize on it. Exclusive stores brazenly hang life-size freeze-frame pictures of the suave executive-in-a-hurry from his or her display ceilings, promising the customer the same air of distinction that is borne by the individual in the picture.

Little electronic innovations such as headsets for your cell-phone offer a cockpit-style convenience so that your hands can be free to operate your PDA and send an email. Even if you aren't flying at the moment, you can still feel like you're flying. All I can say is, "Mayday, Mayday, let me out of this hype." The duty free section of an airport strikes me as the paragon of this concept and how it has made a home for itself in Western culture. There is a certain sensation of eliteness that this section of the airport wishes to bestow on its patrons. It's almost like the glossy walls are whispering to you to indulge in the classy treatment you deserve. It's a self-contained hub in the galaxy of air travel that bears absolutely no resemblance to the real world.

In this hub there are no weather changes—there is no weather at all. There is no time—you're rendered beyond time. Day and night are irrelevant to you. You are within hours of any inhabited point on earth. You are in the antechamber of a luxury vehicle that will thrust you above the clouds at almost supersonic speed to your destination. In this environment you cannot help but feel that you are moving, that you are progressing.... I cannot blame you, but I have to bring you down to earth. Have you ever had the experience where the trip was more exciting than the destination? You're surely familiar with the image of tourists at the airport just before their flight, all perky and chatting excitedly; but then when you fast forward to the actual tour you see them passed out on the bus as it takes them from one boring site to another. This should serve as a stark reminder that going somewhere is not necessarily getting anywhere. The duty free sensation is purely illusion. It tingles the nerves and inflates perceptions, but is nothing more than clutter, our favorite fiend.

Yet more and more people are taking to the skies, running around. The World Tourism Organization forecasts an average of 4.1% growth in world tourism in its vision of the first 20 years of the new millennium. The slowdown of 2001 and 2002 was temporary and travel is already returning to full swing.[2] People are definitely not slowing down.

Well, I am not going to tell you to slow down. I am going to tell you to—gasp—*stop* for a while. The world does enough spinning. You don't have to spin, too. Stop. Take a break, for two weeks. I know you have to go to work, you have to do carpool, and you have to go shopping for food. But you don't have to be the chairperson of the book club, of the school sports committee, of the fundraising committee (I know that's a good deed, but not at the expense of your *self*). You do not have to go to retreats for conventions, to launching parties for new galleries, to networking luncheons, to carnival day on the peninsula, to open air symphonies downtown. For a period of two weeks you will be asked to keep a bare-bones schedule of that which is necessary. Anything beyond that should be either cancelled or postponed. It will enable you to taste a unique quietness, one that will facilitate a proper methodical attempt to build yourself up the right way.

The Greener Grass Syndrome

If I haven't poked my finger enough at pop culture, this is sure to do the trick. Here, I would like to explore the root causes and examine the consequences of a seemingly simple statement that people routinely make: "I'm not comfortable with this situation anymore." Comfortable. Hmmm.

---

[2] WTO's Tourism 2020 Vision forecasts international arrivals to exceed 1.56 billion people by the year 2020, about double the current numbers.

This must be some valuable comfort level, because marriages, friendships, jobs and ideologies take a back seat for its sake. The comment is effectively saying, "Uh-oh, there's a problem here. Can't be anything wrong with me. Must be the situation. Let me change my wife. Let me change my job. Let me change my city, and everything will be alright."

Stop right where you are! Could it perhaps be suggested that discomfort is OK? As we pointed out in the "Cocooning" section, we are not all individual universes. It is not our job to build a shield around ourselves and to maintain a constant comfort level akin to thermostatically controlled central air. Accepting the discomfort is not a sign of weakness. On the contrary, it shows a level of maturity and strength to accept the fact that we may be at fault and that we may be in need of introspection. Through making the correct internal changes we will be effecting real change, and we won't feel the need to run away from ourselves. We won't be so quick to change our spouses if we change ourselves first. The same goes for our friends, our jobs, our homes, our cities, our state. This process requires some braveness on your part to "let go" a little and be prepared to take some blame. (I told you this book was not going to be a walk in the park.)

Other manifestations of the Greener Grass syndrome include the old romanticized concept of going backpacking around the world. There still exists that rare breed of college graduate who is preoccupied with finding meaning (rather than finding money), who launches himself at the four corners of the globe in the hope of "finding himself." When I went backpacking at 21, I was not necessarily motivated by finding meaning, per se, but I did not want to exclude myself from the mainstream credo, since this would call into question my status as an authentic backpacker. Backpacking was definitely a sub-culture, replete with its own set of standards, practices and even language. Even so, as much as I set out to "find myself" so that I could meet the backpacking expectations, I found I was trying to grasp a notion so nebulous it was like trying to grab intellectual jelly.

How on earth was I meant to "find myself" if I really didn't know what that meant? After six months of traveling much of Eastern and Western Europe I came to the conclusion that for me backpacking was really all about the thrill of finding a decent youth hostel and a non-tourist food store so that I could keep under that no-go restricted zone of $10 a day. Perhaps for others it was different, but I quite honestly didn't find myself. Tasting other cultures was pleasant, just like tasting different types of exotic fruits that make you Ooh and Aah and then you move on. When you arrive home, now you are meant to be elated and content because you have found yourself. Yes, found yourself in a lot of debt because now you have to face those student loans you have avoided over the past few months.

Trying to understand who you are does not require you to buy an air ticket or a Eurorail Pass. Right where you are, you can begin the investigation. In the following chapters, I aim to show you how. The Schedule Slimming period lasts for two weeks. Not only will you be asked to slim your schedule as proposed above, but you will be asked to consciously refrain from thinking about switching your environment. Every time the thought pops into your head, "I have to get out of this situation," I ask you to put up a fierce resistance and stop your mind from lifting you up and dropping you outside of your environment.[3]

How Do I Coordinate This Period Together With the Media Fast?

This depends on how you are surviving the Media Fast. If you find you begin the Media Fast and your withdrawal symptoms are mild—you're dealing with it well—then take on the two week period of Schedule Slimming right away. For example, if you begin your Media Fast on Monday and by Thursday you're doing fine, then begin the Schedule Slimming that day and end it a few days after your Media Fast.[4]

If, on the other hand, you find you are struggling with the Media Fast, then don't begin the Schedule Slimming until you are ready. However, at the very latest you should begin it the day right after you have completed your Media Fast. There should be no break between the two periods because then you run the risk of losing the momentum.

These first two steps are aimed at clearing the clutter. Once you're doing that, it may leave you to wonder just what you are going to do with all this time on your hands.

---

[3] I am obviously not referring to those people who find themselves in an abusive relationship which is harmful and warrants immediate outside attention.

[4] See Models of Integration in Appendix I for a bigger picture of how to integrate all the steps of the Diet.

6

Step 3: The Ledger

YOU'VE TRIMMED THE FLURRY OF MEDIA IMAGES. You may also have slowed your crazy schedule. You're alone with your thoughts. What comes to mind? You might find that you're thinking about the TV show you're missing or the email sitting unopened on your computer downstairs. You might be thinking about other people in your life. Things that you were too busy or distracted to think about previously will now come to the fore.

Inner Surgery

Start thinking about yourself, not what you did today or mundane facts about yourself. Rather, how would you describe your personality? How would you define your character strengths? How would you define your character flaws? What things interest you? What things trouble you or cause you pain? What are your goals in life? Are you achieving them? What is your ideal situation? This exercise is best captured on paper. Sit down and write one paragraph about yourself without pausing. Do not write as if you are applying for a clerk position in an accounting office, by recounting your administration experience and skills. Do not write as if you're filling in a census poll by informing yourself who your mother is and who your brother is. Just let your first impression of yourself free flow from your pen or your keyboard. This is something you will disclose only to yourself, so don't worry about letting go. Don't worry about punctuation or about having logical order to your sentences.

A totally honest look at yourself is what we are aiming for. Cutting into yourself is like surgery—it's painful, but it heals you. It treats the root of the problem. Avoiding this surgery (i.e., "It's my co-worker's sloppiness that is responsible for my anger") is less painful for you, but doesn't treat the problem. Don't hesitate to expound on your faults and character flaws. Resist the impulse to be defensive and move your pen onto the next point which is not quite as painful for you as this one. Remember, nobody is going to be reading this. You don't have to justify yourself or provide "sound" reasoning for your behavior. Don't engage in blame transferal. Lay "who you are" bare on the page in front of you. Don't be afraid. Do it.

This exercise should be started towards the end of the second week of your Media Fast, regardless of whether you have begun the Schedule Slimming.

A sample paragraph (although yours could look totally different) reads as follows:

I am witty—sometimes irritating people, I'm sensitive, sometimes to my detriment. I am caring and insightful. It's not the fault of my occupation that I don't make more time for my family—it's my fault. I am condescending. I aspire to be knowledgeable, but I lack discipline...

(I would go on but it's personal and has revealed too much already.)

Although there are a myriad of personality permutations in the world, each with their own nuances and idiosyncrasies, certain elements are typical. These general categories or themes cover many of our individual idiosyncrasies. I have chosen seven categories as basis for a general ledger you are asked to keep for seven weeks. This ledger will contain records of your struggles, successes, and defeats in each area. It is called *The Satellite Map*, because at the end of the seven weeks you will have a sweeping overall impression of yourself.

Day by day, for seven weeks, you will be filling in this map. Please refer now to Appendix II, where you can glance at the structure of *The Satellite Map*. In the coming paragraphs, I will explain how *The Satellite Map* works, so don't worry if it looks to you like a cross-section of a silicone microchip. I know it seems detailed and complex, but then again the human being is hardly simple. Once you have begun filling it in, you'll see how easy it is to navigate. The only difficult part is, and will remain, your daily struggles. Such matters, as you've no doubt come to recognize, cannot be articulated with an instant purchase of human software for $99 or your money back. Yet I hope, through participation in this program, you'll achieve a steady advancement in your overall metaphysical health. You will have insight into your life, into your behavior, into how to have direction and conviction, how to interact with others, and how to achieve a state of happiness and fulfillment that is not superficial or arbitrary.

The Seven Categories:

Each category, explained in more depth in succeeding chapters, is an individual step in the Soul Diet.

1. Order and Fitness.

The maintenance of a healthy body and a structured living environment which provides the right platform for a focus on spiritual growth.

2. Anger Control.

The conscious decision to refrain from anger through understanding its roots and its effects.

3. Speech Control.

Paying attention to the quality of one's speech through recognition of its potency.

4. The Giving Factor.

Tackling strained and confusing personal relationships and employing the power of giving as a methodology.

5. Intimacy

Maintaining a strong, sensitized approach toward intimacy through focus and precaution.

6. Goal Control.

Careful goal selection through meticulous inspection of underlying agendas and motivations.

7. The Happy Factor.

Rejecting superficial modes of happiness and striving for the genuine happiness continuum.

You won't know how to fit all of the intricate pieces of your life into this giant seven-week puzzle until you read further and undertake each step. It is also not possible to grasp the essence of each of the seven steps until you actually experience them.

The Common Denominator

Before we structure the puzzle, we need to reveal the basic principle underlying all seven steps. It is a principle we mentioned in chapter three when we discussed the dual nature of a human being. We explained that much of our day is composed of battles, big and small, between the two souls inside us, the *Nefesh*, the animal soul, and the *Neshamah*, the Divine soul. We emphasized that this conflict is meant to be there. It is the natural state of consciousness programmed into us. Our sole task in this world can be crystallized into one statement:

To let the Neshamah win the battle, so that we may grow. That is the simplified strategy that forms the foundation of this book, and the foundation of our metaphysical health.

We mentioned that our goal is not to live a life absent of conflict, or there would be no possibility for growth. Rather, our function is to deal with the conflict in an intelligent way. The seven steps all involve common sources of conflict. They are "problem" areas known to provide us with the greatest challenges. It's a common perception that since these areas often cause us such dire levels of distress, there is something seriously wrong with our lives. Some even go far as to proclaim their lives worthless. I will say it again, because it can't be said enough: Problems do not mean there's something wrong. It means you're being challenged, which is exactly the way it is supposed to be.

It is the way you deal with each challenge that actually determines the quality of your life. If you deal with the particular challenge in a positive constructive way, you have succeeded, even if the challenge is still there. Even if the challenge remains with you for the rest of your life, if you deal with it appropriately, if you let the *Neshamah* dominate over the *Nefesh*, you will have achieved exactly what you were expected to achieve on this earth.

By critically evaluating yourself in the context of these seven areas of challenge, you will be able to identify which areas need improvement, monitor which areas are being handled appropriately, and determine which areas to make your main focus.

This ledger concept is loosely based on a system presented by Rabbi Mendel of Satanov in his work *Cheshbon ha-Nefesh*, which means "An Accounting of the Soul."[1] I am using different variables than those of Rabbi Mendel, and my ledger does not work exactly the same way as that of the rabbi, but the concept is essentially the same, that of charting one's daily and weekly progress in certain areas of challenge.

Mechanism

How does this chart system function?

One area is presented as the focus per week. Each area occupies one full page, and the page is divided as follows (using Week 1, The Order and Fitness area as an example):

The Umbrella: Names the area of challenge. It is the broader macro concept that encompasses many smaller, more defined particulars.

Subcategories. These are the smaller categories that fall under the umbrella. In this example, the subcategories are Diet and Exercise Conviction; Maintaining Order; Unhealthy Fitness; Unhealthy Order; Punctuality and Commitment Problems.

Nerve Center. This is the specific subcategory you have identified as your most intense or pronounced area of challenge. If equally intense, there can be one or more nerve centers. In the above diagram, the nerve centers are defined by bold type.

Inclusions. These are those personal hard-to-categorize details within each subcategory that relate to your past experience and involve specific situations. "I keep switching diets thinking the new one will help me" is an example of a personal detail that falls under the subcategory of Diet and Exercise Conviction; and "I'm always late for work" is an example of a detail falling under Punctuality and Commitment Problems.

---

[1] Published in 1845 with the encouragement of Rabbi Yisroel Salanter (see Chapter 1, footnote 2)

Umbrella 1: Order & Fitness

SUBCATEGORIES	**Diet and Exercise Conviction** Maintaining Order Unhealthy Fitness, Unhealthy Order **Punctuality and Commitment Problems**	
INCLUSIONS	**SUCCESS?**	I keep switching diets thinking the new one will help me. I'm always late for work.
DAY 1 OBSERVATIONS	✔	I resisted the impulse to buy a new diet book and instead started looking up one I have already tried
DAY 2 OBSERVATIONS	✘ ✘	I only noticed today that I never show up exactly on time for anything. Even when I consider myself to be on time, it's always a couple of minutes late. I miscalculate the amount of time needed to get somewhere on time.
DAY 3 OBSERVATIONS	✔ ✔	I left very early for both of my meetings today, and was surprised to find that I arrived only 5 minutes early both times. But it felt good, I was in control.
DAY 4 OBSERVATIONS	✘	It's difficult to maintain enthusiam for a diet that nobody else is doing anymore.
DAY 5 OBSERVATIONS	✔	I was never so conscious of how inconsiderate it is to be late for appointments. Today was an eye-opener for me.
DAY 6 OBSERVATIONS	✔ ✔ ✔	I really focused today. Clean house, on time, paid bills right away instead of putting them aside.
DAY 7 OBSERVATIONS	✘	Burnt out. I need to work on consistency.

The paragraph you wrote about yourself earlier must be kept handy so that you can plug in those unique details into the diagram for each Umbrella. Part of the function of the ledger is to assist you in transforming the abstract, free-flowing current of thoughts you expressed on paper into a quantified, structured system that you can work with. The paragraph and the ledger are essential. Without the paragraph, you might think mechanically about yourself and omit the more esoteric parts. Without the ledger, your profile remains a collage of complex ideas difficult to grasp.

Each day during that week, you should wake up with the umbrella theme of the week on your mind. As Rabbi Mendel writes for his chart, "Throughout the week, you should say [to yourself], 'When will this event (challenge) occur to me so that I can [overcome it]?'" Thus you will prepare yourself ahead of time for your challenge, an extremely useful tool in dealing with the challenge. It's the difference between being ambushed and detecting the enemy ways ahead on your radar screen.

At the end of the day, you will fill in your chart. Evaluate whether you succeeded or failed in your particular challenges. A ✔ is success and an ✗ is fail. Write your observations about your challenges. Rabbi Mendel writes, "If your original intent was not fulfilled, even partially, consider why. If it was because of a mistake, then try to understand *why* you made that mistake, using your analysis as a means of learning a lesson for the future." [2]

Both the nerve centers and the Inclusions are evaluated as you go along. At the end of the week, tally your ✔s and ✗s and regard carefully your observations. You will be able to identify patterns about yourself that you may have been unaware of previously. As Rabbi Mendel points out, you will be able to, among other things, notice particular days on which one thing happens more than others.

When you move to week 2, Anger Control will be your umbrella and hence your focus. But keep the lessons gained in week 1 as a background presence. Don't worry if you do not succeed in that area, because you cannot be expected to focus on two things at once. But at least you will be conscious of it.

What if the umbrella is not a challenge for me at all? If you have ascertained that there is absolutely no work here for you, you may move on to the next umbrella and your total program will be reduced by a week. However, such an event would be rare considering that each umbrella is so multi-faceted and the fact that even though you may practically succeed in an area, your motivations for those actions are going to be examined and put to the test, as will be explained later.

Regression

In cases where your chart reflects regression in an area of challenge, do not think that this is a bad sign. You might even try to over-correct it—this is also not a good idea. By virtue of the *Nefesh-*

---

[2] From a translation by Rabbi Shraga Silverstein, (Jerusalem/New York: Feldheim Publishers, 1995), 55.

Neshamah relationship it is unrealistic to believe that once you hop on the charts it should be smooth-sailing and your metaphysical health should escalate like stocks in a bull market. Swings are perfectly natural. Not only that, but the regression is itself a challenge. I.e. it is there simply to discourage you. As Rabbi Mendel writes, "Regression is a trial set in [your] way."

That feeling of despondency is the real enemy. It is not so much that you may have failed your challenge that is critical, but whether or not you fight that feeling of despondency. This is a very important principle to bear in mind for any challenge that comes your way across the umbrellas, nerve centers and inclusions. Your task is not to overcompensate but to just keep going at the same pace and not get discouraged.

"Trampled by the Elephant"

Being that the *Nefesh* is the name for the animal soul inherent in us, Rabbi Mendel advises us to be cautious when it comes to our enthusiasm for spiritual growth. Some people are immediately inspired to meet their challenges, charged with a passion they believe will conquer anything in their way. They rush out to the front lines armed and ready, only to find that their excessive zeal has caused them to get burnt out. They find themselves without energy and ironically get trampled by the very elephant inside them that they were trying to trample.

It is important not to get too carried away. In addition, there may be times where the stress of following this diet will get to you, and you will consider giving up. Instead of completely giving in, go the middle route and employ relaxation techniques to deal with the stress: simple breathing exercises, a walk in the park, or more vigorous exercise are well-known ways of reducing stress levels, and there is plenty of literature on that. Of course you are not permitted to go to a movie, surf the Internet, or even read a novel. By relaxing without external stimuli you are refreshing yourself without leaving the diet, and you will find strength to deal with your challenges.

Willpower

As for the strength to deal with our challenges, the subject of willpower receives surprisingly less attention than it merits. If there are resources on it, these generally center around food control, perhaps mentioning a couple of other smoke or drink related addictions too, but not as a subject that should be regarded as a major force in dealing with all facets of our everyday lives. The truth is we should not be surprised at all. Willpower is not an easy tool to acquire. You cannot purchase it. You cannot take it in tablet form 3 times a day. It means hard work, and instinctually we would prefer to either dance around the subject of willpower than harness it, or to create other quickie sophisticated solutions for our lives that don't work.

That being said, willpower must be understood in a broader context. There are many people who admit to the need for possessing willpower but who are not motivated to develop and use it. I believe there is very good reason for that. Willpower is there to meet a particular challenge or goal. The virtues of that goal, however, are seldom defined, and seem to be assumed. For example, as indicated in the next chapter, the goal of dieters is to lose weight. That goal's underlying motivations are rarely questioned. Nobody quizzes the dieter as to his or her purpose in losing weight. You can imagine the response to this question, and the ensuing dialogue as follows:

Dieter: What do you mean, why do I want to lose weight?

Quizzer: I'm asking you why it is important for you to lose weight.

Dieter: Because I look terrible. I want to look good. (Frowns)

Quizzer: Why do you want to look good?

Dieter: What's the matter with you? Stop asking such silly questions. I want to look good because…I want to…I don't know…I want to look good.

Quizzer: You haven't answered my question.

Dieter walks off.

Not a very successful interchange. But the point is made: People set goals which require willpower but they don't necessarily dwell on the deeper purpose of those goals. Rather, the goals' inherent values are taken for granted and the achievement of those goals gets immediate and premature focus.[3]

For willpower to operate successfully, a proper deliberation of the proposed goal must be performed. Once there is a profound purpose, all that energy spent on maintaining willpower becomes worthwhile. If the purpose is poorly defined, why should we bother with all that hard work? We see little reason to keep up such a rigid regiment. So let's go back to that dialogue with the dieter. Why does she want to look good? The answer is, as you now know, that meeting the challenge of dieting results in personal growth. Our goal becomes attaining metaphysical health, which is a deeper, more meaningful state of being, and, as we will see in the next chapter, maintaining a healthy body is essential to maintaining metaphysical health. In other words, the ultimate goal of losing weight is metaphysical health. Losing weight becomes a means to an end, rather than an end in itself. This concept applies not only to weight control but to all of the goals we set, from making money to making marriage work. It gives us a much more rooted fundamental purpose in meeting the challenges of the "daily grind." Moreover, when our motivations are defined in this way, the "daily grind" itself becomes appreciated, even pleasurable, because it is understood as the means to a greater end.

Willpower Insider Information

The *Chosen Yehoshua*[4] remarks that being creatures of habit has its benefits. When we are about to embark on a particular path to deal with a challenge, the task seems formidable. And, indeed, the

---

[3] The subject of setting appropriate goals gets full treatment in Chapter 12.

[4] Literally *The Power of Joshua*, by Rabbi Yehoshua Heller of Telz, Jerusalem 1998, 16.

first few days or weeks or months are difficult to get used to, and one imagines that the level of difficulty will remain at the same consistency throughout. The truth is we get used to things, even difficult struggles. Dealing with the struggle becomes a habit, and the inertia can carry us forward. The author advises that one should bear in mind before beginning a regimen that the burden is going to get easier than what is initially experienced. This helps eliminate a false impression of what the future holds, and helps to build willpower. Thus, before resolving to control your anger (Chapter 8), remind yourself that the excruciating difficulty you will experience in restraining yourself initially will become less severe as time goes on, because you have developed a habit of anger control.

Should you tackle the challenge head-on? *Michtav M'Eliyahu*[5] points us to the incident in the Torah of the Binding of Isaac. In this incident, God commands Abraham to bring his son, Isaac, to be offered as a sacrifice on Mount Moriah. The purpose of this command was to test Abraham's allegiance to God, that he would not hesitate to perform the will of his Creator even if it made no sense to him. As Abraham is about to perform the sacrifice, he is stopped and told that it has been a test of loyalty. The Midrash informs us that along the way to perform the sacrifice, Abraham's inner voice had tempted him, trying to get him to doubt his mission.

"Where are you going?" it asked him, trying to get him to contemplate just what it was he was about to do.

"To pray," he replied.

"For what does someone who is about to pray need materials to start a fire?" the voice persisted.

"Maybe I'll be delayed and I would need these materials to cook food."[6]

What is Abraham achieving with this seeming self-deception? He was not on his way to pray at all. What he is doing is deflecting the attack. When we are presented with a challenge, the Midrash is teaching us, we should not engage it head-on, rather go around it and avoid it. Abraham gave an answer that stalled the voice inside him from drawing him into battle. The answer was not true, but it was fueled by sincere motivations. It's OK to be cunning with the voice of the *Nefesh*, since the entire purpose of the struggle is to defeat that voice.

If we do meet that challenge head-on it becomes a power struggle and we run the risk of losing. Thus, when you're suddenly overwhelmed by a desire to shirk your work responsibilities to go to see the latest *Shrek!*, it's better not to tell yourself, "How can I do such a thing? I'm working," because

---

[5] Literally "Letters from Eliyahu," a compilation of teachings of Rabbi Eliyahu E. Dessler, (Jerusalem: Sifriati, 1997. [1963]), II. 46.

[6] Tanchuma, Vayera, 22.

you have now entered the battle zone with your Nefesh, and he has a whole repartee of tricks up his sleeve. Rather, tell him, "Ok. I'll go, but just give me five more minutes here." After those five minutes, see if you can get away with another 5 etc....After a while, a business call comes in, and before you know it, that voice has retreated in defeat.

In a similar vein, Rabbi Mendel advises that at the onset of a challenge, "nip it in the bud."

"When it is possible to remove oneself from the source of the sensation, the intellectual spirit which can see ahead, can overcome the strongest desires by dealing with them in their first stages."

This is another method of circumventing a large-scale battle with yourself. If you know that you get too judgmental and critical when you see how other parents behave with their children, don't look! After you've looked it's difficult to be armed and ready for battle. If there are two ways to walk to work, and one of them has a doughnut store that is nothing more than a sugar factory, walk the other way! Don't think you're strong enough to win the battle head-on. This is where the Torah's approach differs from some contemporary theorists who advocate exposing yourself to your tests and challenges so that each time you overcome the challenge you strengthen your immunity to it. I do not recommend you follow that advice. The *Nefesh* is a giant, and we are midgets. Don't intentionally mess with it, because it has hormones and brainwaves that can swallow you up in an instant. If it starts up with you, that's all well and good because that's your challenge, but if you start up with it, you're asking for trouble.

Willpower correctly harnessed, charged with the right motivations, paves a path to dealing with all the umbrellas of our ledger. The first umbrella, though, is particularly significant since it, itself, is a fundamental aid to willpower....

7

Step 4: Order and Fitness

Fueling Up First.

IF YOU DECIDED TO START A MOVING BUSINESS, and anticipated carrying heavy goods on a daily basis for several hours at a time, you would probably consider getting your body into shape and getting your health into order before you embarked on such an endeavor. If you just went into it head first, you would run a much greater risk of strain and injury carrying that sleeper sofa up three flights of stairs than if you had prepared and groomed yourself for the job beforehand. Similarly, if you decided on a whim to run a marathon because that alluring image of breaking the winner's tape with your hands in the air would make a nice addition to your scrapbook, you'd actually want to go around the block at least a few times to see if you're up to the task. You might discover that running 26 miles when you're not ready for it is not quite as tenable as when you are. When it comes to preparation for physical endurance and strength, such training is considered the norm. Its necessity is so keenly understood that some might deem it common sense.

Less attention is paid to the methods of preparing ourselves for our spiritual battles which occur to every human being on the planet, every day, several times a day. It doesn't matter about your vocation; whether you are a mover, a long-distance runner, a Wall Street broker or a Key West bartender, we all experience the battles that we have identified thus far as the intersection of the *Nefesh* and the *Neshamah*. Would it not make sense to be at our fittest and most alert when confronted with the lures of the *Nefesh*, as it attempts to steer us from the steadfast path to which we have committed ourselves?

If you have resolved to spend more quality time with your children, wouldn't it help to feel like you have the energy to do it? And I don't mean merely sitting quietly with them in a garden swing reading from a five-page laminated picture book. I mean the type of active rough-and–tumbling that kids need to experience with their parents once in a while: playing tag, wheelbarrow, and ride-the-donkey. These are moments that can create a magical bond that remains permanently etched in the child's memory. ("I remember my father used to….," a 40-year-old says with a broad smile and twinkle in the eye.)

The *Nefesh*, not to be defeated so quickly, argues that you've had a long day. You really do want to play with your kids but right now you could do with a cup of coffee as you rest your feet and read the newspaper. Now you're thrust into battle. If you're physically unfit, you eat poorly and your environment is in disorder, it becomes much harder to win the battle. You are more likely to go with the flow, the flow of the *Nefesh* dominating your decisions, telling you to go the most comfortable route as you have done with your physical state and your environmental conditions. If, however, you have committed to eating and living healthily, to maintaining as much order in your immediate environment as possible, you now come into the battle better equipped. Being fitter creates more energy, and being organized helps you to prioritize better and helps you to schedule in the important activities with your children along with everything else.

Similarly, if you have resolved to refrain from anger in all your dealings, particularly with those closest to you, you will fare much better with a good night's sleep. If you are already on edge before you've finished your first yawn of the day, the *Nefesh* has received a powerful boost in its mission of sending you over that edge. The same situation that you are able to deal with calmly when you are well rested, can trip you up when you are not. This may seem obvious, but the workings of the *Nefesh* are rarely fleshed out, and in studying its mechanics we might be able to take a deeper interest in controlling it.

In a study supported by the National Institute of Health, Dr. Roy Baumeister, of Florida State University, found that self-control used up important physical resources and that sleep was one way to replenish those resources. "Most forms of self-regulation failure escalate over the course of the day, becoming more likely and more frequent the longer the person has been deprived of sleep."[1]

So keeping the physical side of you healthy and strong is an aid to keeping the metaphysical side of you equally healthy. However, this is where we will deviate from the mainstream approach to physical fitness and health. And this is a theme we will repeat in each of the umbrellas: *Physical health is not an end in itself, it is a means to metaphysical health.*

Once you have a noble goal, there is meaning to your exercise methods and nutritional madness. The artificial miles trekked on your basement exercise bike at 5 in the morning are actually leading you to a place beyond your physique—to a level of maturity of understanding. You view your body as a mere tool. It is your means to victory in the everyday battles you encounter. This seems like such a subtle distinction, but when you actually approach your regimen with this attitude you will notice a big difference. As it is most commonly experienced, the unspoken attraction of the gym circuit or the aerobics class is that you will end up with a great body, and that's it. Yep, a great body. The fantasy of what that will do for you is much greater than the reality. Do problems melt away with a slim waistline and a couple of pumped-up biceps? The overarching sensation you're left with after your newly defined muscles are glistening in the sun is…. *flatness*. Is that it? Wait, there must be more.

Yes, there is more. But only if your intention from the start is not to bask in the halo of your superfit body. When you go into it with the premise that you want a fit body so that you can

---

[1] Eurekalert.org – A service of the American Association for the Advancement of Science; Public release date 19 Feb 2003.

function better and therefore face your daily challenges and battles better, then you start to feel that are you going somewhere. You are bypassing the flatness on your way to your metaphysical goals. Those hours battling the cheesecake and the bench press are leading you to your destination, boosting your ability to meet your challenges.

It's Not the Diet. It's the Conviction

Working on a fitter body lands us in the same vast colorful market as everyone else doing the diet thing. Although we have just stressed the importance of the overarching metaphysical goal of our diet or exercise program, we nevertheless still have to utilize those options out there that will enable us to achieve it.

Let's begin with dieting. Which one should you choose? Here, again we are opening ourselves up to the information invasion. I probably don't have to list for you the endless variety of diets out there with all their dazzling permutations of calorie control, revolutionary anatomical discoveries and digestive obstacle courses, but needlessly to say each one will categorically claim that this is the diet that will finally work for you.

And they are probably all right.

According to an article by Gay Riley, MS, RD, CCN of Netnutrionist.com, the US population spends approximately 50 billion dollars per year on weight loss, including low calorie foods and beverages, which is 50 times the money spent by the United Nations for Hunger and Famine Relief! The article maintains that one out of every 3 Americans is on a diet.

Now comes the clincher: 95% of the people gain back all their weight within the time it took to lose it. So it turns out that the diet will most probably work. The question is whether or not the dieter will maintain the conviction necessary to sustain the weight loss. This is an entirely separate issue from working out which diet triumphs in effectiveness over another. Most diet books can recount for you story after story of impressive weight loss statistics—those inimitable before-and-after scenarios that wow the reader into immediate action. Reading each one will convince you—well, now I *really, really* have found the right diet, and those first few moments of burning inspiration do in fact melt away the pangs of hopelessness and desperation. Whether it's a mathematically sound carbohydrate-fat-protein equation or a zoom-in focus on fruits or fibers, there is a sense of elation at having finally found the winning formula.

That's Day 1. And also Day 2, 3 and 4. But the nature of things is that after a while, perhaps two or three months, that initial glow begins to fade. The impregnable resoluteness is not so impregnable anymore. Your cravings, on the other hand, remain as strong and healthy as ever. This is one of the amazing facts of life: You can get bored of your fantastic diet, but you will never get bored of a fantastic slice of chocolate cake. With further weakening of your defense system and greater indulgence in the forbidden, the diet slowly (or even quickly) becomes a thing of the past. At this point the intellect would attempt to diagnose the problem. What happened over here? Now just because we are speaking of the intellect, it doesn't mean that we are eliminating our old friend, the *Nefesh*. Because even though the *Nefesh* represents the more instinctual physical side of us, it also is extremely adept at developing whole paradigms of false philosophies designed to justify our actions.

So, the *Nefesh* argues, the problem must have been the diet. Yep, I don't know how I could possibly have gotten so caught up in such a strict regimen that virtually denied me the pleasures of life. Surely I should knock some sense into my head and take on a diet that is much less demanding, a diet whose basic tenet is everything in moderation—a little bit of this and a little bit of that, and you know that's really the way God designed us…yada, yada, yada. That is the compelling closing argument of the *Nefesh*. And what if the initial diet was, in fact, one of everything in moderation, of which I am now bored? Well, the *Nefesh* points out, I can't possibly have expected success where I make a mediocre attempt at dieting. I have to go all the way when I'm dieting. It's all or nothing. If I don't break away from mediocrity then I can't expect to make a dramatic difference in my life…yada yada yada. That is the *Nefesh*'s compelling closing argument from the other side of the bench.

Do you now appreciate how brilliant a lawyer you have inside of you? The guy is undefeatable (or almost). All of this is, of course, sweet music to marketers' ears. They are behind you 100% in your thinking that you just haven't found the right diet yet. Because if everybody realized that the problem is not the diet itself, there would be no need for another diet book to hit the shelves ever again. There would be no new secrets unveiled, no new number one New York Times Dieting Bestsellers inhabiting our billboards, no new cash cows grazing on consumers' greenbacks. We would all sigh collectively, and say (looking down), "No, no…That's not the problem. Another diet book is not going to help me."

We would all gather the resolve to examine the core of the problem, which, according to the above statistics does not appear so difficult to identify: the fact that almost all the people who embark on diet programs gain back their weight. This would lead us right back to our subject of willpower, the ability to sustain the momentum. And, remember what we said about the key to willpower? The important thing is asking ourselves *why*. Why would we go to such great lengths to prime our bodies? Why would we deliberately subject ourselves to deprivation? And we would answer that the underlying goal of metaphysical health is what motivates us. A great-looking and feeling body is only the means to fulfillment and not the end. Armed with such purpose, we would approach dieting as we would approach all other challenges in our lives, as mere catalysts for our spiritual growth. We would reject the notion of starting another newly brandished, multi-colored miracle diet every time we lost momentum. Rather, we would encourage ourselves to fight the real battle of self-avoidance, that which prevents us from listening to the real statistics that almost shout at us: *You're missing the point! It's not the diet, it's the conviction.*

This would all be true if everybody would admit to the real problem. It would be a type of colossal group confession, the sort that would invoke a little embarrassment, a little guilt, but mostly a lot of relief. Exposing ourselves to what we really have known all along, but were too afraid to act upon, is actually a cathartic process. Of course it's tough, because it means we're choosing to face the challenge rather than embrace the more comfortable alternatives, but at the end of the day it provides us with much greater peace of mind than when we succumb to those alternatives.

To get the whole world to do this ain't gonna happen. But you, the individual reader who is serious about genuine change, can open yourself up to the idea that the real focus is your own willpower, not the flashing neon diet revolutions spinning off the press.

To help you make this transition in perspective, you could take a few minutes out to write down your reasons for embarking on the diet. One very important thing to remember is that this does not mean you're free to choose any reason your heart provides. Your heart may tell you that you're dieting because you want to look good on the beach in the summer or because you want to fit snuggly into the yuppie market, cruising at the forefront of trendiness. These are not quite stepping stones to metaphysical health. They are your heartstrings being played like a harpsichord by the barrage of media imagery. They are the very stuff that illusion is made of.

Your focus should be on maintaining your physical health as a means to being a better person. We mentioned that fueling up first on our physical resources serves as an aid to being metaphysically strong. Bearing this in mind will be a great asset in your battle against the *Nefesh*, especially considering that this will be the common denominator in all of your struggles. It's almost like team work. Once you have the same foundation for approaching everything, you build up a strong resistance to any one of the challenges coming your way. Without this inner "support network" you have to rely on fighting the dieting challenge with one lone arsenal of dieting willpower. Think about how demanding it is on yourself if you are resolute about your weight loss program but allow yourself free reign in all other aspects of your life. It's like trying to swim upstream with only one arm working furiously against the current and the rest of your body relaxed with the flow of the water. You're asking too much of yourself. You are one glaring bundle of inconsistency. If you follow this program, however, and apply our principle to all the umbrellas of this book, you have a team inside you working together to achieve discipline and metaphysical health.

This approach applies equally to exercising. There are, naturally, a whole slue of stay-fit work-out programs, clubs, centers, tracks, and state-of-the-art machines ready to assist you in your assault on your languid body. Similar to the dieting phenomenon, there are countless new improved secret formulas for body mastery being revealed to the world faster than you wallet can empty its coins. Exercise magazines, articles, cable TV programs, videos, CD's, and DVD's continuously dig up new ways you can twist and turn your body into shape. Again, they all pretty much do the trick. Exercise magazines would most probably go out of business if everybody realized that Issue One, Volume One of a physical fitness magazine contained all you really needed to get into shape. *The trick is being able to stick with it.*

But they're not going to go out of business very soon. So, you are left with your own personal fortitude in the matter, which, as you now know, involves grouping this battle together with all of the others, keeping your ultimate metaphysical health as the backdrop for your pursuit of physical fitness. You are getting fitter on the outside to help you get fitter on the inside.

The nature of exercise is that stamina and endurance is gained only by much strain and perspiration. The strain experienced differs from the strain of dieting. While the strain of dieting often entails feelings of deprivation and resentment, the strain of exercise can be a painful but pleasurable experience at the same time for some folks. It's the old *I can conquer anything* instinct that provides a sense of personal victory to one's struggle. In fact if there was, hypothetically, a way to achieve physical fitness without any strain, many people would actually lose interest. So one would think this type of attitude is a noble one, deserving of accolades. Sorry, but I'm going to have to take issue with this seemingly benign motivation. (You might be sighing at this point, and understandably so. Bear with me. It'll be worth it in the end.)

The kind of pleasure experienced with the physical strain of exercise is risky. It can easily feed the ego, trumpeting your ability to defeat your own muscles. It can even border on narcissism. There is always at least one person strutting around the gym with his arms extended like an eagle coming in to land because apparently he is so pumped up he is unable to put them straight against his sides. There is always at least one aerobics star offering you endless unsolicited counsel on why your movements are all wrong. It is easy to fall into the trap of trying to prove your invincibility as an athlete. This kind of pleasure as you toil will most likely cause you to deviate from your altruistic goal of metaphysical health. It will much sooner become an end than it will remain a means. This is something to keep in mind, especially when the culture of the age can actually promote that elitist approach to exercise. Advertising in this area actually lures you to the image of your physical prowess, awakening in you fantasies of dominance over your body and entry into a super sleek social club. It's tough to go against the grain. But, again, it's possible to fight this battle in conjunction with all the other umbrellas of this book because, as we mentioned above, you have a "team" working for you.

Recommendations from Maimonides

Once you have prepped yourself for approaching dieting and exercise with the right kind of perspective, you can now go ahead and choose the right type of diet and exercise program. We've mentioned before that there are myriad choices out there wherever you look, so it's not necessary for me to provide you with these resources. However, what I will share with you is an approach to healthy living—tucked away in the sacred teachings of the philosopher Maimonides who died eight hundred years ago—that has never made the rounds of conventional marketing outlets.

Maimonides, one of Judaism's foremost commentators on the Torah, penned several guidelines, from the Torah's perspective, on how to maintain one's physical health. Before he actually details the various instructions, he reminds us, "If a person's focus is merely that his body and his organs should be whole [i.e. functioning], that he should have children who are able to perform their tasks and exert effort where necessary, this is not the right path. Rather, his focus should be that his body is whole and strong *so that his Nefesh be straight [i.e. directed] towards the knowledge of God.*"

Only when one's underlying motivations for keeping fit are directed towards metaphysical fitness, does the concept of exercise and fitness achieve its purpose.

The actual list of instructions is quite lengthy and substantive. I've highlighted some of the points you might want to bear in mind when you develop your health plan. Remember, some of these points are not for immediate practice; but serve as long-term ideals that, with time, can be achieved. Do not overwhelm yourself at once with a fitness regimen that can take a lifetime to perfect. Slowly does it.

1. *One should eat only when hungry, and drink only when thirsty.* This may sound all too obvious, but if you give it more than a fleeting thought, you will realize just how much we eat and drink outside of these parameters. Our old friend the media, for one, does a splendid job of convincing us to dive into something sizzling just for the taste of it, just for the low price of it, or just for the heck of it. Then there's the refrigerator trap. It's a trap simply because it's there, and as you walk past it your hand swings out to open it and peer inside, even if nothing could possibly have changed inside it in the five minutes since you opened it last.

2. *One should not eat until his stomach is full. Rather he should stop at three-quarters of satiety.* This can take a lot of restraint, requiring you to leave some of the food that just begs to be eliminated off the plate. After all, there's no greater compliment to the cook than a nice clean plate, right? Well, if you're worried about hurting your host's feelings, then at least when you are eating alone and feeding yourself, there is no reason why this principle should not apply.

3. *One should drink only a little during the meal. Once the food has begun to digest, one may drink what is necessary to quench one's thirst (but no more).*

4. *One should not eat until he has thoroughly checked himself that he doesn't need [to use the restroom].* Elsewhere, Maimonides reiterates that which is mentioned in the Talmud—the principle that one may not delay one's needs even for one moment.[2]

5. *One should walk, or perform other such exercise until his body is warmed up before eating. In addition, if one has the opportunity to wash in hot water after the exercise, that is even better. After washing, he should delay a little and then begin eating.*

6. *One should remain seated in one place while eating. He should not move about until the food has begun to digest.*

---

[2] This principle applies whether or not one is about to eat. Here, in the context of eating, Maimonides seems to advise added precaution to make sure one is clean.

7. *One should get eight hours of sleep.* Maimonides advises that those hours should be calculated so that they end just before sunrise, i.e. one should go to sleep approximately eight hours before the next morning's sunrise, so that one can get up just before the sun "gets up."

The concept of getting a head-start on the day is encapsulated in the prose of King David's Psalms,[3] *I will wake up the morning.* This forms the basis for the opening words of the Code of Jewish Law[4] which prescribe forming a focus of one's mission during the day even before getting out of bed.

8. *If eating both light and heavy foods together, one should eat the lighter food first.* For example, chicken should be eaten before red meat; eggs before chicken. (Does that answer which came first?)

9. *One should eat seasonally appropriate foods.* In summer months, one should eat cool and refreshing foods, and in winter months, warm and spicy foods. Although this seems like another common-sense prescription, it is enforcing the idea of not subjecting your body to stress and strain, rather than simply ratifying your natural cravings.

10. *One should avoid eating foods that cause constipation.* Retaining waste can cause illness.

Maimonides adds a rule of thumb: as long as one is fully active, does not eat to complete satiety and maintains a soft constitution, one will likely be healthy and strong, no matter what one eats!

Order Outside and In

Rabbi Yisroel Salanter would say that having an ordered exterior environment is an aid to creating order on the inside. When you condition your mind to a pattern of disciplined action, the idea of applying it to your persona is not so foreign to you. When you're used to acting with alacrity to get those bills taken care of instead of putting them aside until their due date, it will also be easier for you to act with alacrity to get off the Internet and have a real conversation with your spouse.

The concept of inertia generally has a bad reputation. It is most commonly understood as a detractor to growth, but in this instance you can harness it to your benefit. Just as when you're sitting down for a while there is an inertia keeping you from springing to your toes, inertia can work in the opposite direction if you allow it to: Inertia becomes momentum. When you're already revved up to make changes in your external environment, you'll find that your energy can spill over into other areas, as if you are coasting on your inspiration. Now that you are moving, there is a natural force keeping you in this pattern, and you can just go with the flow.

---

[3] 57,9.

[4] Known as *The Shulchan Aruch,* compiled by Rabbi Yosef Karo (1488–1575).

Instead of fighting to make changes around you, you will actually find it hard to stop making changes. Just picture the homeowner armed with a loaded feather duster around spring-cleaning time. All dirt particles begin to quiver and tremble in the path of this single-minded dirt eliminator. And very often, once the dust and the cobwebs have been crossed off the list, the energy is still bubbling to do more, to dig deeper and tackle weight issues, relationship issues, to bleach and detoxify all that has been hanging around in the dark abandoned corners of the conscience.

Thus, making changes inside you can be jumpstarted by starting with the simpler external clean up. An ordered environment will include a clean house, an ordered office and (yes, I'm afraid) even a clean car. If you can't keep everything inside your head (some people can), you might make a schedule to make sure you can deal with the laundry, the car pool, the doctor's appointments, the meetings. Even more vital than that is updating that schedule. Making rough estimates by squinting at last month's schedule could be the beginning of the slippery slope.

You will also have to venture into that ominous tangled jungle that in prehistoric times was a place to put your car. The garage has come to serve as the ultimate black hole for all your clutter. It's an untampered sanctuary that houses all your IDWIL's.

What's an IDWIL? I just made it up. It means "**I**'ll **D**eal **W**ith **I**t **L**ater."

Admittedly, sorting out the garage can be a monumental task that can take a long time, certainly longer than the week allocated here for order and fitness. What's important is to make a start. Begin this week. The very act of opening that door for the purpose of removing, not dumping, is a significant step toward untangling the jumbled junk. And if you ever had doubts about how much our culture embraces niche market product innovation, there are now companies out there formed with the express purpose of helping you to clear your house or office of clutter. They have names that go something like "Organize Yourself" or "Clear it up," addended with the obligatory .com or dot something else. (Not to mention that I am just as guilty with a web site like Souldiet.com). It's somewhat ironic that the obsession with niche marketing is what has contributed greatly to the problem of clutter in the first place.

Be that as it may, these companies do exist; and if you find it too overwhelming to tackle the mess in your house or office, it may be wise to make use of their services. Again, I'm going to throw in that caveat that will reappear so many times that by the end of this book it will probably stain your brain like an advertising jingle: You must examine *why*. Getting yourself and your property in order may be a positive step but it must remain a means, not an end. The end, to reiterate, is metaphysical health. You are straightening things up not simply because a clean, ordered environment is easier to live with, but because, as Rabbi Yisroel Salanter advised us, it is a means to clarity on the inside. This will provide meaning to your cleaning spree, helping you avoid that feeling of wasted time and effort spent cleaning something that's only going to become dirty again. How many homemakers out there view their cleaning rituals beyond an endless cycle of tail-chasing? The spotless floor, the folded laundry, the paid bills, the washed dishes, the cooked dinner are not exactly achievements frozen in time. It's more likely to be frozen for the next five minutes or so before the moment melts and you have to do the whole thing again. And again.

But if attention is focused on the process involved, that it is a facilitator to mental clarity and metaphysical health, that it triggers a desire to achieve an ordered state of being, then you're not chasing your tail. Your goal, no matter how diverse the steps seem in their respective applications, is the same overarching sense of clarity shared by all the steps of the Soul Diet.

Unhealthy Fitness, Unhealthy Order

Another consequence of a single-minded focus on fitness and order—as an end rather than a means —is that it becomes an obsession. And we're not just talking health consciousness here; we're talking an entire lifestyle.

All of you have at least once had a conversation (even a heated one) with someone who talked endlessly about the detrimental effect of sugar, processed foods or dairy products for what seemed like hours. Not that the scientific evidence for these arguments should be ignored, but it should be taken in context and not become your life. What you consume should not consume you. Yes, take note of the warnings—with a modicum of suspicion, I might add, as the theories are constantly changing. But don't let them rule you. Do you recall the parody of the airline pilot in chapter 2? Well, that's just the point. You can get lost in the quagmire of mechanical functions and forget your destination.

Health and fitness clubs have added fuel to the fitness fire by emphasizing a sense of self-actualization through their style of music, décor, and marketing. There can be found, inside these doors, an almost palpable sense of competitiveness, accompanied by the inevitable feeling of inadequacy for all those who don't quite make the grade. All of this totally misses the point. It is, perhaps, a modern reincarnation of Ancient Greek body worship that finds its focus in a netherworld far removed from the course of the Soul Diet. Yes, it is correct—even an obligation —to keep oneself fit, but don't go building fitness empires for yourself where you intend to spend much of your time and energy.

How do you know if you are fixated? Obsessed? When your two hours of gym every evening after work are non-negotiable, while your aged father's request to visit him is; when you weigh your food choices down to the ounce but everything else in your life is a mess; when you insist that your family should eat the way you do, and if not, well, you just won't eat out with them anymore; when you won't even consider looking for a marriage partner until you are in a certain desired physical form or condition; when preservatives in foods bother you more than how little time you spend with your kids.

I think you get the picture. This area is a particularly difficult one to address, since it has a sophisticated defense counsel armed with seemingly flawless logic. After all, you are a person with a mission—you are furthering health consciousness, changing attitudes of indifference to vital physiological issues, bringing your body to optimum levels of performance that allow you to maximize your life experience. On challenging this line of reasoning, you have to be prepared for your own resistance (if you are not feeling it already). You will likely feel a measure of annoyance in facing this challenge. There will be many words of protest that you will string together in the most articulate of ways, but they can be directly translated into simple language: "Leave me alone. This is my life. This is my world and I believe I'm doing the right thing." The words "I" and "my" appear quite a few times in these translations. This is because in its raw form, an over-emphasis on health and fitness is just another example of self-indulgence. It is well obscured by its veil of sophistication, but it is self-indulgence nonetheless. That being the case, this kind of obsession is an obstacle to a balanced perception of the self and clouds the path toward metaphysical clarity.

If this is your challenge, this week you will attempt to cut down on the amount of time and energy you spend working on your body. Of course you will feel the need to divert this energy into something else, but for that you will have to be patient until you reach Chapter 12 where you will be ready to define your goals. If you can't wait and you're finding it too difficult to work on this imbalance without having a substitute goal in hand, one way of dealing with it, though drastic, is to imagine that you are given only a short time left to live on this planet. It will help to convince you that the end goals of life supersede the means. The notion of a deeper purpose will loom larger than the myriad details in which we lose ourselves.

Of those very unfortunate people who actually do receive the grim news that their lives are in the balance, many do experience a sensation of urgency to zone in on the ultimate purpose of existence, rather than continue in a sleep state of monotonous routine. It is a heightened state of awareness of life, an acute sensation that something must be done, something must be achieved. Admittedly, many are largely unprepared and untrained for such sentiments and find it difficult to latch on to exactly what it should be. Some go for sky-diving, mountain climbing, exotic world travel and other adrenaline-charged activities, but others are at a loss for how to satisfy that deep-seated urgency to make the best of the time left. Hopefully, through the course of this book, we will succeed in decoding some of those blurred parameters.

Thank God, most of us have our lives ahead of us. But does that mean we should deny ourselves this epiphany? If we are feeling restless without our fitness fad and we have to wait until chapter 12 to actually go ahead and prioritize our goals, at least for now the goal of being less obsessed with the details can be more immediately accessible through this insight. It can serve to prepare us for what will become more formalized in chapter 12. Use it as a temporary solution to help you shift away from your obsession. It will remind you that there is a bigger picture, that you have to zoom out of the pixels in order to observe the image. So, at least for this week, stop reading up on the dire effects of John Doe toxins and Joe Blog Preservatives. Cut your exercise routine in half and leave your calculator out of your calorie computing. I'm not telling you to sit back and let the carbs roll in. Keep being healthy but just don't obsess.

It's about Time

Philosophers have frequently mused about the concept of time, eagerly pursuing and delineating its frontiers and its limitations. However, for most people, time is an entirely practical thing. "What time is it now?" is heard more commonly than "What is time, anyway?" The two approaches seem completely divergent, each one adopting a different focus. At the outset it seems improbable that answering the question, "What time is it now?" with the question "what is time, anyway?" will win you much favor with the questioner who has a plane to catch.

Well, as you have probably guessed, I am going to create a point of intersection between these two approaches: an understanding that those practical aspects of time—punctuality and scheduling—derive their importance from exploring why time is meaningful to us. There are those people who struggle to be on time and struggle to create a schedule, and those who obsess with being on time and cannot think of living outside a schedule. Both groups can benefit from an analysis of how time fits into our lives.

We are going to tread lightly on a well-worn path of questions that usually meander my way. Many people ask, "If everything is predetermined, where is there room for free choice? God knows what we will decide even before we decide it." This is not our subject. However, in presenting a possible resolution to this perplexing problem, we will hopefully gain some insight into the concept of time.

I generally reply that the question itself is faulty. The question does not even begin. In formulating the sentence, the questioners used the word "before." God is beyond time. The concept of "before" or "after" puts no limit on God by definition. "Before" and "after" may very well exist simultaneously in one capsule.[5] Since God is not bound by time, it makes no sense to ask, "But God *already knew*…." The problem is we get trapped by our assumptions right away. We so quickly take the concept of time for granted that we cannot possibly fathom an existence beyond it.

In any case, what we Soul Dieters gain from this little philosophical interlude is the idea that time is a creation in itself, inserted into the universe purely for the benefit of its inhabitants. Time is therefore an important tool, one that, harnessed correctly, can help us progress towards metaphysical health.

Thus, the celebrated concept of Time Management and its accompanying seminars and workshops receive an important preface in our book: Time should not be a tool for egocentric advancement, for achieving self-centered maximum efficiency. It is that part of creation intended to help us with real, balanced growth—our metaphysical challenges and struggles. Just as a super-fit body helps you to face your personal challenges, when you are punctual and organized you also have the ability to face your challenges—not merely your rigorous work schedule but how you control your anger, your speech, even your sexual impulses, all the umbrellas of this diet. Rather than helping you become a well-oiled machine zooming toward self-aggrandizement, time management should be understood as a means to *overall* metaphysical health.

---

[5] This concept is represented in the tetragamatron of God's name, which is a hybrid of the Hebrew words for was, is and will be.

Let's illustrate this with an example: One of your primary marketing objectives at work is to develop loyalty within your existing customer base so that you can stay one step ahead of your competitors. When a customer calls or emails, you have resolved to be on top of it and have the fastest turn-around time in the West.

The time manager in you informs you that to make this practical you will have to prioritize your responses, ranking them based on how much they make you $mile. Now it happens that you get personal calls or emails, some of them from your spouse, your parents, your friend in need, and your immediate thought is, *I'll get back to them when I can. I'm just swamped right now,* because although your friend in need makes you smile, he doesn't make you $mile. You will discover in detail the dangers inherent in this approach when you go through some of the other umbrellas of this book, but it becomes quite obvious, even at this point, how easy it is to use time management in a destructive way. On the other hand, if time management enables efficient use of time so that you not only get more work done but improve your relationship with those close to you and concentrate on attending to those elements in your character that could use fine-tuning, then you are using time for its intended purpose.

Time is also the partner of fitness and health in helping to remove you from a state of disarray. The *Nefesh*'s favorite habitat is disarray. When it has you there, it can so easily push you in the wrong direction because your defenses are down. How much resolve could you work up to refuse something bad for you if you have no idea which end is up? This is why time is there to help you set your day according to a defined schedule. It's basically a sorting machine that, efficiently used, could bolster your immunity against your weaknesses. Always remembering your ultimate goal of metaphysical health will help motivate you to be strict with time.

At the same time, be careful with that strictness that it doesn't develop into an obsession. Obsession with time is again missing the point, even if you're set on improving yourself all-round. There are those who find themselves rating others by their capacity for time management because *I am always on time, so why can't they be*? It's so easy to slip into that judgmental phase, sending you skidding all the way into chapter eight and Anger Control, chapter nine and Speech Control, chapter ten and The Giving Factor where some heavy maintenance awaits you.

As with all the umbrellas of this diet, the way to ensure you have the correct perspective is to always bear in mind that goal of metaphysical health as your ultimate motivation. By definition, metaphysical health rejects disorder at the one extreme and rejects self-worship at the other extreme. It's that balanced outlook that will take you all the way through this book to The Happy Factor and beyond.

Fill-in

This is where you fill in your personal areas of challenge relating to order and fitness on The Satellite Map. They are the "Inclusions" we spoke of in the previous chapter.

The following are examples or ideas for Inclusions that you could use or build on if you relate to them:

- I can't stop eating chocolate
- I don't get enough sleep
- I keep switching diets thinking the new one will help me
- I'm always late for work
- It drives me crazy when others are late

For our sample chart below, I selected two Inclusions from the above list: *I keep switching diets thinking the new one will help me*, and *I'm always late for work*, and filled in the chart based on these two challenges.

Try to fit whatever your Inclusions are into the following sub-categories, really a digest of what we uncovered in this chapter:

- **Diet and Exercise Conviction:** the ability to recognize that it's not the diet or exercise program that's the problem—it's the conviction.
- **Maintaining Order:** the ability and resolve to sort and classify items and information
- **Unhealthy Fitness, Unhealthy Order:** an obsession with health, nutrition and fitness.
- **Punctuality and Commitment:** Striving for a balanced approach to Time Management.

Those sub-categories highlighted in bold type (which you can circle in red ink) are the Nerve Centers, your most profound areas of challenge. The two Inclusions in this sample belong to those Nerve Centers.

Umbrella 1: Order & Fitness

SUBCATEGORIES	**Diet and Exercise Conviction** Maintaining Order Unhealthy Fitness, Unhealthy Order **Punctuality and Commitment Problems**	
INCLUSIONS	SUCCESS?	I keep switching diets thinking the new one will help me. I'm always late for work.
DAY 1 OBSERVATIONS	✔	I resisted the impulse to buy a new diet book and instead started looking up one I have already tried
DAY 2 OBSERVATIONS	✘ ✘	I only noticed today that I never show up exactly on time for anything. Even when I consider myself to be on time, it's always a couple of minutes late. I miscalculate the amount of time needed to get somewhere on time.
DAY 3 OBSERVATIONS	✔ ✔	I left very early for both of my meetings today, and was surprised to find that I arrived only 5 minutes early both times. But it felt good, I was in control.
DAY 4 OBSERVATIONS	✘	It's difficult to maintain enthusiam for a diet that nobody else is doing anymore.
DAY 5 OBSERVATIONS	✔	I was never so conscious of how inconsiderate it is to be late for appointments. Today was an eye-opener for me.
DAY 6 OBSERVATIONS	✔ ✔ ✔	I really focused today. Clean house, on time, paid bills right away instead of putting them aside.
DAY 7 OBSERVATIONS	✘	Burnt out. I need to work on consistency.

8

Step 5: Anger Control

Playing Anger Geography

A FRIEND OF MINE WAS ADVISED BY HIS THERAPIST to get himself a punching bag into which he would divert much of his pent-up frustrations. He duly hung it from a tree in the yard and engaged in frequent punching sessions, just as the doctor ordered. Since there was no damageable property —human or otherwise—at the receiving end of his blows, such "healthy expression" of anger was viewed as harmless. All he was doing was having a boxing match with an item specifically designed to release frustrations. So what could be wrong with that?

The first issue deserving our attention is the idea that diving deep into one's anger is a good way to rid oneself of it. Actually, the *American Psychological Association* reports nowadays that such an approach not only does nothing to subdue the anger but also is clearly "a dangerous myth."[1] Perhaps this compares to raiding the candy store and stuffing yourself with sugar so that you won't crave sugar later on. Of course the reality is that merely one taste brings back all those cravings; you'd be better off without it.

Secondly, such a theory holds that one can play "Anger Geography," that is, you assume that anger itself is not a problem—it's where that anger is aimed that is of prime concern. By this reasoning, if your anger targets people or property that will suffer as a result, that's one thing; but if the anger is not causing any harm then, by all means, express it as a way of relieving your tension. The underlying sentiments behind this attitude are indicative of a much broader societal tendency to judge the dangers of a negative behavior or character trait not by its intrinsically harmful nature but merely by the impact it has on others.

Q: Why is it wrong to steal?
A: Because others will be deprived.

---

[1] APA online, Office of Public Affairs.

Q: Why is it wrong to kill?
A: Because another person's life is lost.

Q: Why is it wrong to have an affair?
A: Because you've breached another's trust.

By implication, if there was some way (hypothetically, of course) to commit these things without hurting anyone, then there really would be nothing wrong with it. Or would there be?

In this book we've been opening our eyes to the reality of metaphysical health. If you are in the midst of a program aimed at stability and refinement of your character, a sudden turn toward negativity would be just the curveball to throw you off balance. Putting a negative trait into action will do this, regardless of the consequence. Even if you somehow manage to get away with no damage, entering the parameters of theft, murder and adultery immediately creates a mindset that is in itself harmful; not necessarily to others but to yourself as your thought patterns are redirected toward an unsavory cause. Your goals shift. You take on the persona of a violator of moral standards —you embody that person.

Similarly, anger is harmful by itself even if there's no one there to receive your verbal or physical punch; even if this is touted as a healthy way to "let it all out." Ironically, by getting into the mindset of "letting it all out," one gets worked up: the adrenaline pulses freely and the mind is immersed in the anger and frustration that is meant to be disposed of. Some people pull faces and even growl, grit their teeth and become enraged, their faces turning scarlet red. Here one has dipped into a realm of anger complete with its characteristic thoughts and impressions. An angry person's thoughts and impressions of life are generally darker, more cynical than that of a calm, controlled person. The irony is that an angry outburst—instead of providing the immediate relief we expected—carries a feeling of entrapment to that anger, the feeling that one has succumbed to something primitive.

What pattern have you noticed here that has surfaced at each stage of our diet? That battle, of course, which is the quiet war inside you. The *Nefesh*, seeking immediate gratification, is at odds with the *Neshamah* which understands the longer-term impact of following the *Nefesh*. The *Nefesh* charges, "Let that anger flow." The *Neshamah* responds, "It's sweet and delicious now, but then I have to face the music." Battling anger is no different than all of our other struggles. The desire to fall into anger is a test of our resolve. Overcoming anger is a victory that helps us maintain our metaphysical health.

Self-worship

What is at the root of this feeling, anyway? If we are to tackle anger, it would be helpful to come to grips with its essence. Of course it's difficult to overcome the enemy if you don't know how the enemy operates.

There is an intriguing teaching of the sages that compares one who becomes angry to one who worships idols, a strictly-forbidden practice in a monotheistic faith. What would be the reasoning behind this? The angry person has a single-minded focus which, admittedly, can seem like an advantage in our cluttered world. The words swimming around in the head of the angry person are not half-baked. Just picture an actor telling someone on screen to "get out of my sight!" Nostrils would flare and eyes would be scorching, and there would be no mistaking the enunciation of the actor's words. Simple, forceful, raging. That person has direction. Just the wrong direction!

Rabbi Tzadok[2] explains that idol-worship is a manifestation of the desire to control. If you can declare your god, you are selecting one according to your tastes and your personal needs so that even your "higher authority" is in fact a puppet in your hands. It is a profound expression of the ego: Yes I have a boss, but one elected according to my needs. Similarly, anger is a symptom of inflated ego—the sense that "I" have not been served fittingly. According to *my* life-view, things should have gone this way and they went another. Anger and idol-worship share a clear, undiluted manifesto: I want things to go my way, and no one should dare spoil my equilibrium.

Such self-absorption will most certainly lead to frustration, since it is virtually impossible that "the way I see it" will always be honored. There will always be a time when things aren't running according to plan, and the juices will begin to boil. In fact, we spend quite a substantial portion of our day (assisted by our old nemesis, the media) in dreaming about our future, a seemingly innocuous pursuit that appears to be a healthy exploration of our imaginative powers but is in reality an absorption in hype that almost never materializes. Much of our anger stems from a deviation of the way we imagined things.

And from where does our imagination draw its strength? From the motto of follow *your* heart, live *your* dreams, be the person *you* always wanted, get what *you* want from your relationship, achieve the wealth *you* deserve. Accomplish the impossible! When all this gets drummed into your psyche, where is there room for someone else's ideas that don't quite intersect with yours? It's ruining your grand designs. If you pick up a book that guarantees you tremendous riches by following a detailed strategy, does it allow for an earthquake that might ruin your real estate investment? Or, more subtly, does it leave room for the possibility that your wife may not be as enthusiastic about your ideas as you are? In such a case, do you try to fit your wealth strategy into your marriage or do you try to fit your marriage into the wealth strategy? Well, someone who has been indoctrinated with the "me" philosophy all their lives, will prove hard to bend. Yes they would expect their marriage to fit into the wealth strategy, and even begin the argument at home with, "Honey, I'm doing this for you, for us…."

The argument heats up when the "plan" meets resistance. Everything went so smoothly in the book. It was so simple. Now she is "ruining" things, and all you want to do is create a better life for her. *How ungrateful,* you think.

Oh, yes, the *Nefesh* is that devious. In this area, the lawyer inside you works overtime. It dresses up self-absorption as the humanitarian element working for the benefit of mankind. Anger results

---

[2] Rabbi Tzadok HaKohein of Lublin (1823–1900) in his book, *Resisei Layla.*

when the "lofty" goals take a head-on hit. This may be upsetting to read, because in some sense you might be feeling mislead by the marketing gurus who have encouraged you to spend your hard-earned dollars on an essentially faulty stack of cards. Living your dreams, it turns out, just might make you into an angry person; or if you started off angry, magnify your anger even more so. This is both ironic and sad.

This week I will ask you to examine those moments when you feel anger coming on. If your thoughts tell you, "Someone or something is ruining things for me," try to think a little about that, dissecting exactly what causes you to stir. Think about how you acquired that plan or philosophy of yours that is being disturbed. Did you expect everyone and everything around you to conform to it? Did an article, theory, book, film, person or moment of solitude suddenly inject you with an explosive plan for your advancement or for the advancement of those close to you? Did you decide right away to implement this plan because it would be unthinkable to question it? Take, for example your philosophy on child-raising. Try to trace the argument you are presently having with your spouse about child-raising methods to the time, perhaps many years ago, that you developed your understanding for the best way to raise a child. It could be two years ago when you attended the lecture of a world-renowned psychologist. It could be five years ago when your father sat down with you before you got engaged and gave you some wise tips. It could be twenty years ago when your father lost his temper with you and, well… suffice to say that you swore there and then that as a parent you would never ever do *that* to your child.

Back to the present: Did you ever consider that the other person in front of you cannot see the epic, biographical video of your experiences that plays in surround sound in front of your eyes?

Is it right to automatically expect the other party to tow your own party line? You could hardly be blamed if you did because the media moguls have encouraged you to build a fortress around your ideals, to celebrate your own thoughts, to follow your own dreams, to conquer the world with your own unique perspectives. What if, under intense and sometimes agonizing scrutiny, you were to discover that you were, ahem—wrong! Not obviously wrong; just subtly so. Because you discover that at the core of your motivations is self-indulgence and you simply dressed this up with altruistic objectives, all in keeping with and buttressed by your urgent and cunning advisor, the brightly colored life-coach manual that is so tangible that it might as well be on your bedside table. Even if I were to grant you that you were objectively correct, based on the wealth of your experience, and your intentions noble, could you justify anger as a response to someone who doesn't see it that way?

I don't mean to imply arrogance on your part. The simple truth of the matter is that the actual moment of inception of your plan, idea or theory of how things should run is often overlooked and assumed to have existed for all time; a truth you assumed—without you ever having to discuss it—automatically built into the fabric of your relationship. This is not necessarily a symptom of arrogance but rather a lack of awareness and a misunderstanding on your part. Often we are shocked to learn that the basic tenets of the private moral frameworks we daily carry around in our heads, principles we may assume to have existed for all time, are actually *not* universally accepted by everyone around us.

Not infrequently, after many years of marriage and gritting her teeth at her husband's grueling, wholly engrossing work schedule, in the midst of conversation a brilliant light bulb virtually blinds this woman with its luminescence:

> *He does not and never has meant to desert me; he simply does not understand my feeling of desertion. He has never realized why I would feel deserted; he thinks he has been my valiant savior for fulfilling his role as my provider. He has never had the tenets of my personal moral constitution built into his head. I simply assumed that he saw it, instantly, from my perspective. And you know what, he must have his own personal constitution of ideas and theories swimming around in his head, things I am totally unaware of. I wonder what I unwittingly do to him that blatantly violates his constitution yet gets unanimous approval by the governing board in my department!*

And a parallel light-bulb might well appear in his vision:

> *It's not that she doesn't appreciate what I do for her. She appreciates it tremendously. Yet she has never understood my perception of the work ethic, of what is required, to get things done.*

Watch how, with such satisfying realizations, the walls of tension, anger and resentment begin to crumble.

You will thus have this week to explore those areas that you've long presumed to be irrevocable truths and that you assume everyone around you would naturally respect if they were worth their salt as mortal mensches. You will try to isolate the areas of your anger and investigate its origins.

So, if you discover that your ideals are backed by altruistic intentions, just that you assumed everyone else would automatically understand them—and are now suddenly finding out differently —then work on gently explaining to others where you are coming from. And start to hear out the others' positions. At the same time, if you realize you have unfairly imposed a life goal on someone else and that on closer inspection it turns out at its core to be nothing more than your own self-indulgence, this is the time to begin reevaluating what you have adopted as a game plan.

I did not say this diet was easy.

Visiting their heads

The basic principles of the above approach are expanded upon in the teachings of Rabbi Zelig Pliskin[3], who invites us to actually imagine what goes on in the heads of others who are causing

---

[3] *Gateway to Happiness*, (Jerusalem: Aish HaTorah Publications, 1983), 207.

us anger. This is not simply an exercise in developing respect for a point of view other than yours. It enables you to immerse yourself in a different mindset the way you would if you were visiting a foreign country and trying to get a sense of its culture. What are the customs here? What are the norms? The only way to find out is to taste it yourself, to pretend you were sharing the mind of the other person and seeing life through foreign eyes.

With such an approach, you might develop new insights into a personality you were sure you had all figured out. By a way of illustration, try to analyze some of the decisions, thought patterns and ideas that you follow in your own everyday experience. How often do you do or think something that you find irritating to yourself? How often does your own opinion on something make you angry? How often do you set goals for yourself that infuriate you? In most cases, the answer is not often at all. Actually, the question sounds preposterous—how could you possibly be angry with your own opinion? That's because you see your side of things so clearly, so obviously, you could swear it was Federal Law by which the entire nation abided. You may not even think of it as your *opinion* that you happen to be quoting and not indisputable fact. Why, you may ask, would I argue with fact?

Similarly, your neighbor has a crystal clear vision of his opinion, and cannot for the life of him understand your anger and frustration at something he understands to be as real and tangible as the shirt on his back. Thus the idea is to try to access his cozy paradigm and ask, what drives this? What is fact here? What is the fuel for this engine room? What you learn may surprise you greatly.

Tunneling with Talk

What if someone has "done you wrong" and you can't possibly fathom any justification for it even if you try to view things from his planet? Someone created a lie about you, for example, and spread it maliciously and vigorously so that you are now facing unwarranted claims from several people who are now about to terminate their relationship with you because of it. You've exhausted your mental capacity for visiting this person's mind and understanding how he operates. You can't do it. The fact that he grew up in a dysfunctional family and has a warped sense of justice is not helping you to calm down much.

In his methodical decoding of several verses in Leviticus, Nachmonides, another famous commentator, reveals a step-by-step recipe for confrontation with those who have wronged us. The famous command to love one's fellow as one loves oneself is preceded by verses that seem unrelated at the outset, yet in actuality are necessary precursors to this ideal.

The verses[4] line up as follows:
1. Do not hate your brother in your heart.
2. You shall surely rebuke your fellow [so that] you may not bear sin.
3. Do not take revenge, and do not be vengeful.
4. You shall love your fellow as you love yourself.

---

[4] Leviticus (19,7).

Nachmonides[5] identifies a pattern:

Goal #1: *Do not hate your brother in your heart*, when he has wronged you. How do you achieve that? *You shall surely rebuke your fellow.* You should ask him why he has done such-and-such a thing to you. Rebuke here does not automatically infer an aggressive stance. What is critical is to question the wrongdoer in such a way that you show your goal is nothing other than to return to the equilibrium of not hating him in your heart. The moment you indicate that your goal is to prove him wrong, you will lose everything you are attempting to gain. People can very quickly sense the tone behind the question, and will instinctively become defensive if they feel attacked. On the other hand, if they sense you are trying to restore the relationship, it is very possible they will become responsive and even apologetic. This is why the verse continues to say, *so that you may not bear sin.* Which sin? The sin of hating him in your heart. In other words, rebuke him in such a way that you will no longer hate him anymore for what he has done. That should be your goal.

Once you have achieved this, be careful that you *do not take vengeance*, because it is possible that though you no longer hate him in your heart you nevertheless are reluctant to forget what he has done; and if the situation should arise that he asks you for your assistance, you find yourself refusing.[6] *And do not be vengeful.* This is more subtle. Even if you accept his request for assistance, you do so with a touch of condescension, as if to communicate that "I would never wrong you the same way you wronged me." Only then, after passing all these steps, is it humanly possible to reach goal #2: to *love your fellow as you love yourself.* You've gone through a thorough process to achieve this. Without the process, fostering a strong connection with someone who has just wronged you is quite unfathomable.

Bear in mind that these are ideals that may take a long time, perhaps several years or even a lifetime to achieve. After all, I am right now providing instructions for dealing with people who may have seriously wronged you. Yes the steps are effective, but they are not achieved overnight. This does not mean, though, that we can't begin work on them this week. At least we have an idea of how to progress.

I Can't Stand It

There is a type of anger that has triggered the formation of whole organizations, fueled international movements and created office jobs for thousands of people everywhere. This is the anger sparked by injustice. Social or humanitarian groups often derive much of their passion for their cause from a reaction rooted in anger. Clearly, while the world has many understandable problems, acts of nature and the like, there are some human-induced problems that really, really tick some people off. Enough that they might decide to join a rally or lobby group, or start a rally or lobby group, or even dedicate the rest of their lives to addressing the particular problem. What about this type of anger?

---

[5] Ibid.

[6] Rashi ibid.

You might expect this paragraph to be really short because this time the answer must be simple. I mean, how could anger at world injustice be wrong? Surely there is nothing to talk about here.

Well, as usual, I am about to make things complex again, simply because they are. First we need to recall the issue we raised with the talk-show concept, where dense and intricate subjects are trivialized and downsized to fit snuggly into the commercial capsule. Broad, sweeping subjects that require vast amounts of "boring" study and investigation in order to be fully appreciated are given the sensationalist treatment for adaptation to the thrill-hungry listener who is all-too-often just waiting to be outraged. Even the most mundane, innocuous news story can be transformed by a verbal make-up artist into a breath-taking commentary on human indecency. This type of outrage we might call "pop-outrage," where a person will develop an instant fury over a perceived injustice without having ever adequately researched the subject or even having entertained the possibility of dissenting opinions. This is where anger at world injustice is indeed wrong; the label of injustice has been issued far too prematurely. What can emerge is a pumped up balloon of idealism, and if you prick it….

The Los Angeles Times[7] describes a protest initiated by American activists against the retailer *Toys R Us* for opening branches in South Africa during the era of Anti-Apartheid sanctions. What the activists did not know, or investigate beforehand, was that a South African businessman was the real culprit, simply copying the *Toys R Us* logo for his own stores. The real *Toys R Us* had nothing to do with it. This is a case of obvious misinformation. Yet in the heat of the protestors' ire, the fact that they might have been completely misguided did not occur to them. They saw something, and they reacted. The adrenaline solidified into a platform of protest and away they went.

Most cases are not as obvious as that. They are more likely to be gray areas riddled with complexity and subtlety. That means that a thorough study of the facts is required long before standing in line for the soap box. How is it possible to be an armchair commentator on international crises that require college courses just to learn the basics? Now let's say you've done your homework. You really do know what you're talking about, and your position is justified. Will I finally allow you to be angry? If not now, when?

Well, sort of. Of course there are injustices, but here, again, we're going to have to dissect this. Enter the *Nefesh*. What does the *Nefesh* serve up when you have been issued a license to anger at world injustice? It plants the idea in your head that you (and your group) are surely the sole fighters for justice in a world that just does not understand. Suddenly you become aware (thanks to your *Nefesh*) that you are the magical light in a dark, dark world that lets injustice ride by. Your *Nefesh* is careful to omit that this is a recipe for self-righteousness. Before you know it, you find yourself riding a crest of self-importance because you have touted yourself as one of the rare perceptive ones. You use every opportunity to speak your mind: at work, at social functions, during special down

---

[7] Bob Drogin, "Leggo My Logo! Battles Rage over U.S. Trademarks in South Africa," Business PART-D; Financial Desk; *The Los Angeles Times*, July 29, 1995: 1.

time with your spouse. And you can't stand it when someone is not on the same page as you. It fuels your indignation. As you may begin to imagine, this type of anger has surreptitiously derailed you from your track towards metaphysical health.

On the other hand, I will concede that where you have taken your anger and channeled it into a purely proactive, well-thought out plan for the betterment of society, where you have absolutely no interest in placing yourself on a pedestal, nor any plans to use your cause as a means to your own self-importance, you are definitely doing a good thing. There are people like this. Just make sure you are one of them.

Angerless Anger

In addition, there are times where anger may very well be an appropriate plan of action. The thing is, it has to be just that—a plan of action, a premeditated, carefully executed response in which you have no intention of becoming angry on the inside, you're just displaying it on the outside. By doing so, you're providing that extra weight sometimes necessary to enforce an idea that deserves a certain level of respect.

There was a very prestigious Torah scholar in my school in Jerusalem who was always gracious and humble in my dealings with him. To me he appeared no more than a well-learned teddy bear who had a giant, very pliable heart. Then I was told that once a new kid who was not yet familiar with the protocol of due reverence for highly regarded teachers, threw his arm around the rabbi's shoulder as if he were leaning on an old pal from high school. The rabbi turned ever so slightly to the young man and said in a sub-zero tone, "I am not your friend."

The same man whose smile would light up the room and whose singing voice would make spirits soar, did not hesitate to deliver a message that would make a stomach sink. His intention was to instill the idea of respect for one's teachers in this young man, purely for the young man's benefit. And the key point here is that the rabbi felt no resentment, either. And a very remarkable thing happens when you show anger but don't feel it. The other party senses and understands right away that the anger is not real, that you are not scalding him with hot molten lava spewing from your core. He can sense that, on the contrary, you are able to maintain a very strong and secure sense of serenity that remains completely undisturbed by the tone of your voice. This is where he begins to respect you. There is an immediate appreciation for the ability to see beyond the moment and to resist the petty instincts to become embroiled in an ego-driven tug of war. He can see that your goals are higher than the average instinct-driven fighter who defends himself, sometimes needlessly, to the death.

In fact there is a beautiful irony that emerges from your behavior: Maimonides[8], in discussing the concept of displaying anger without feeling anger, points out that your intention in displaying any anger at all is strictly to help the other party get back on track. Your interest is not in proving

---

[8] *Hilchos Deos*, Chapter 2, law 3

that you are right and that he is wrong. Instead, you want the other person to succeed and sometimes this is the only way you can get your message across effectively. As strange as it may seem, you actually can come across as caring deeply for the other person. You're taking a strong interest in his development rather than standing idly by and letting him continue to slide along on his course of self-destruction.

This concept is clearly illustrated by the tone of voice we often employ when teaching or disciplining very young children, especially when they unwittingly endanger themselves. "No, no, no, Michelle," the voice admonishes, resolute yet loving. "Don't you ever, ever stick your fingers in the outlet. That is very, very dangerous. Do you hear me?" It is very unlikely that a bystander would accuse the parent of selfish, ego-driven anger, as if the parent were saying, "Michelle – you are wrong, I am right." Obviously the parent has nothing other than the well-being of the child in mind. The display of anger is a tool of effective communication that would hopefully leave a strong impression on the child to ensure her protection in the future.

Similarly, albeit a much more difficult task, this is where angerless anger is permitted in the context of dealing with adults or older children. It is not at all easy to ensure that your anger is a superficial tool for their advancement when all the strings of complex adult interaction start to get entangled with your motivations. There's no inclination to get defensive with a toddler's reasoning. As soon as the level of reasoning begins to climb to within range of yours, however, that's when your battle stations start to activate themselves and you find it difficult not to lose that control you had before.

Keeping such advancement in mind becomes a formidable task. This is why angerless anger is a skill that needs to be harnessed. It's so easy to fool yourself that what you're feeling is not real anger. The reaction of the other person is your litmus test. If the other person senses a personal attack, it probably is. You cannot stand there for half an hour insisting that your anger is based in love while the veins are popping out of your head and the other person is in tears.

In summary, on such matters it is better to be safe than sorry. But if you can eventually master the art of angerless anger it is a very effective means of expression.

Fill-in

This where you fill in your personal areas of challenge relating to anger on The Satellite Map. They are the "Inclusions" we spoke of in the last chapter. The following are examples or ideas of Inclusions that you could use or build on if you relate to them. Earlier in this chapter I asked you to think of the very origins of your viewpoints and opinions so that you could understand the foundations of your anger. List those insights here, in the Inclusions. For example:

– My parents always spent money freely, which left us in inextricable debt. That is why I get upset over my wife's spending habits.

Other fill-ins could be:

- I feel no compulsion to stem my anger when no-one is around.
- I get very annoyed when all I get is everyone's answering machines.
- I get impatient with people who would actually vote for certain politicians.
- I constantly think that I am one of the only people in this house/ business/ administration who has my head screwed on right.

For our sample chart that follows, I selected two Inclusions from the above list: *I get very annoyed when all I get is everyone's answering machines*, and *I constantly think that I am one of the only people in this house/ business/ administration who has his head screwed on right*, and filled in the chart based on these two challenges.

Try to fit whatever your Inclusions are into the following sub-categories, actually a digest of what we uncovered in this chapter:

- **Anger Geography:** Expression of "harmless" anger that can lead to an angry attitude
- **Self-worship:** Anger that results from an insistence that things run your way
- **Blinkered Vision:** Inability to entertain thought systems other than your own, or failure to consider possible causal factors for your own thought system
- **Self-Righteous Protest:** When seemingly justifiable protest can lead to inward focus and righteous indignation.

Those sub-categories highlighted in bold (which you can circle in red ink) are the Nerve Centers, your most profound areas of challenge. The two Inclusions in this sample belong to those Nerve Centers.

Umbrella 2: Anger Control

SUBCATEGORIES		Anger Geography **Self-worship** Blinkered Vision **Self-righteous Protest**
INCLUSIONS	**SUCCESS?**	I get very annoyed when all I get is everyone's answering machines. I constantly think that I am one of the only people in this house/business who has his head screwed on right.
DAY 1 OBSERVATIONS	✔ ✘	Although my boss didn't e-mail me what I wanted when I wanted it, I was able to contain my anger when I realized it was a demand to see things my way. But then when I saw him later I could not stop the feeling of resentment.
DAY 2 OBSERVATIONS	✘	I actually yelled at a fellow committee member, using the word "incompetent."
DAY 3 OBSERVATIONS	✔ ✔	Today I was able to come out with an apology AND a compliment for the person I yelled at yesterday, even though I felt every part of me resist it.
DAY 4 OBSERVATIONS	✘ ✘	I knew my brother was at home and STILL he wasn't picking up the phone. Not only did that make me angry, but I know he had answered my sister's call earlier because she told me she had called him. Now I was furious.
DAY 5 OBSERVATIONS	✘	I just did not feel up to battling my anger with incompetence today.
DAY 6 OBSERVATIONS	✔ ✔ ✔	OK—progress! I offered to help another committee member implement her suggestion rather than react with indignation because the suggestion wasn't mine. Then, when she smirked, I didn't react! I couldn't reach my cousin at the time we agreed to talk, but, bouyed by my convictions, I calmly tried again until I could.
DAY 7 OBSERVATIONS	✘	I had a headache and was not in the mood again for dealing with incompetence.

9

Step 6: Speech Control

Words do break my bones

ONE COULD IMAGINE THE EXPRESSION "sticks and stones may break my bones, but words will never hurt me" as a response created in sheer defiance and denial of a troubled past, as a shield from all the years of verbal abuse. *I've set up barriers, so you can't hurt me now.* You could even imagine it with that childish jingle appended by "na-na-na-na." There are many misleading and mistaken little gems of wisdom that have wound their way down to our ports of conscience, but this one has to rank with the most preposterous of them all. How could a living human who has ever come in contact with other living humans proclaim that words do not hurt? Even if there is that segment of the population who insist they are thick-skinned and don't care one way or another, their skin is nevertheless not so thick as to be impenetrable. There could always be just those words by just the right person at just the right moment that would pierce one's armor and go straight to their heart. And remain there for years.

The irony is that very often a wound inflicted by sticks and stones has a greater chance of being healed than one inflicted by words; and it generally heals faster, too. A broken leg caused by a bike accident might take six weeks to heal; an insulting remark caused by a heated argument might take several years to heal, even after reconciliation. An outburst of, "I hate you," in any relationship, particularly in a marriage where it's not blood that secures the bond but love and respect, may cause an irreparable wedge, a line that plays over and over in the mind even when things have calmed down and the affection has been restored. And yet in many instances the utterance was never meant—it was simply an arrow fired by the cogs of an angry mind. There may have been no truth to the hate at all. But now it has been spoken. The best way to solve this problem is to never get into that angry state in the first place. This is why before this current task we had a week of anger management as a preventative measure. There has to be a will not to ever get to a point of anger when you will say things you don't even mean. Perhaps the most lethal of words that could be uttered in a marriage is an unintended warning of "divorce" in the heat of the moment. That is a fissure that is extremely difficult to mend. The overarching perception now is that the marriage is headed downhill, and the couple will have to go to great lengths to restore the marriage to a positive image.

With all of this talk about the power of words, it behooves us to investigate why it is that words have such a penetrating effect. We are often both surprised and confused by the impact of our own words. Analyzing the roots of speech and its power might give us some direction along our path towards metaphysical health.

Cosmic Power

Words were used to create the world. It is easy to do a cursory reading of the story of Creation in Genesis without ever stopping to ask questions. Even if you're only on day one of creation, though, your mind should be brimming with questions and observations. Let's start with God's command to create light. "And God said, Let there be light. And there was light."[1] Wait a minute. To whom was God talking? There was no-one else around. And why does He need to announce what He is about to do? He is the Creator of the world—He has no need to announce it. Why not simply say, "God created light"?

A somewhat mystical answer to the question draws on an examination of the Hebrew term for "word" and the term for "thing." Both are comprised of exactly the same Hebrew letters.[2] When God used a word, that word itself became the thing! The word crystallized into the object it was describing. God said, "Let there be light" and immediately as he spoke those words—"And there was light." God's words about light became light. This very profound teaching gives us insight into the cosmic power of speech. It was speech that really formed the basis of matter as we know it.

Do you remember back in Chapter 2 when we explained the meaning of being created in the image of God? We mentioned that all human beings have a power to create and destroy as a microcosm of God's power to create and to destroy. Now, in dealing with the creative power of speech, we can begin to understand the responsibility endowed us as bearers of the gift of speech. We have to be exceedingly careful to create with our speech, rather than to destroy.

When we use speech in a positive way, we are building things the eye cannot necessarily see. Just as we spoke about the damaging aspects of speech, there are constructive words that once uttered can wittingly or unwittingly turn another person's life around. The Talmud,[3] for example, recommends that we not take the blessing of a simple person lightly, since any blessing issued has potency. We are so accustomed to token greetings and wishes being dispersed indiscriminately that we hardly value them as expressions of any real meaning. Lines such as "All the best" and "Be well," and in particular the flagship of American commercial interchange, "Have a nice day," are hardly given any serious reflection. They are viewed as no more than obligatory tag-ons to polite conversation. In truth, each of these good wishes can actually affect the course of events. If we would take seriously the idea that our words are powerful, with the potential to create and

---

[1] Genesis (1, 3).

[2] both share the same three-letter root, ד ב ר.

[3] Megillah 15a.

to destroy, then it follows that all things said with intent, no matter how trivial they seem in the scheme of things, will have a definite effect.

I remember clearly the moments I spent with a particular rabbi in Jerusalem who is generally regarded as one of the foremost Torah scholars of our time. Every day people line up at his door seeking his counsel and his blessing. When it was my turn, I began telling him of my hopes and my plans, asking him for his blessing and his prayers. After asking me only a question or two, he wrote my name down and told me he would include me amongst the multitude of names in his prayers. As for the blessing, he said but one word, "Success!" and smiled.

At first, as I turned to leave, I felt disappointed with the brevity of his blessing, especially as I had poured my heart out in quite some detail. And then it occurred to me after a while that people who value how they use every word, who are exceedingly careful with their speech because of an acute awareness of its power to create and to destroy, understand that if you're going to say anything, you mean it 100%. If you're genuinely wishing someone success, you're not merely dropping pleasantries in order to meet the standards of etiquette. Every word is infused with intent. If the rabbi wished me success, what more would he have to say? It wasn't an introductory formality to a long-winded speech that characterizes our product presentations, our political party conventions, or the acceptance speeches at the Oscars. Rather it was a statement made with conviction, concise and expressive of exactly what he wished for me.

In contrast, rambling on and on is a convenient way of spewing empty words so that they sound meaningful, without ever having to mean what you say. The less we value the power of speech, the less importance we place in choosing our words carefully. And when I say choosing words carefully, I am not talking about crafting our sentences to satisfy political correctness, rather the ability to restrain ourselves from potentially harmful statements, choosing instead to spell out the words of encouragement we truly feel but hesitate to express. Those three words, "I love you" should not be reserved only for when its easier to say them, as when you're about to leave for work and you're halfway out the door so that your voice dissipates with the falling rain outside. Calling the person over for no other reason than to express this phrase is much more powerful and memorable.

There are also types of speech that on the surface appear innocuous or ingratiating but that in the long run eat away at relationships. Sarcasm is one such animal, appearing as nothing more than a series of fun-filled jabs meant to keep the relationship fresh and alive. But we are humans, and even a joke tinged with hurtful sword-pricks eventually starts to tear away at the tender membranes that hold people together. What typically happens is that one party starts to laugh a little less each time until she starts to voice protest, to which the other party responds with, "Aw, come on. You know I was only kidding, right?"

"I guess," is now the diluted response of the injured party who doesn't quite understand the hurt herself. The point is, it can only go on for so long before the wounds start to appear; what began as a harmless form of entertainment has now led the relationship to be due for an overhaul before it really gets into trouble.

Gossip and Slander

The Torah repeatedly warns against gossip and slander, more often than for most other commandments.[4] This kind of emphasis can only mean that those of us who think it is merely commendable to refrain from such speech are not quite getting the point. Just because we cannot directly touch and see the damage caused by gossip does not render it a minor infraction. Similar to the crystallization of speech into material form that we said occurred in the process of Creation, we should picture the words we speak about others taking shape and becoming an entity, a real existence that occupies space in the world. Entire conversations, sometimes even entire relationships are centered on gossip. Have you ever felt the difference between a conversation that has gossip and slander as its focus, and one that steers away from negativity to concentrate only on the positive? You may notice that the former has considerable immediate appeal, drawing you into the juicy scrutiny of other people's lives. But at the end of the conversation you may notice an empty feeling, almost like a hangover from your naughty binge. The latter, on the other hand, may be considered dry or bland since it fails to dip into forbidden territory. Many ask, "But if I can't talk about other people, what could I talk about?" They cannot contemplate having a stimulating social conversation that does not indulge, at least once, in some form of judgment or comment about a third party. But at the end of the latter conversation, which has involved nothing other than positivism and productivity, there is a sense of achievement, that something good was accomplished, even though the conversation itself might have lacked the dazzle and allure of a gossip-soaked interchange.

In this arena, the *Nefesh* implores us to delve into the juicy parts, and the *Neshamah* urges us to maintain a dignified conversation. It therefore feels so easy and natural to explore the faults of others. We all know, though, how difficult it is to talk about our own faults. Yet while we delay in accusing ourselves, our tendency is to accuse others very quickly. Our *Nefesh* and *Neshamah* are constantly in court about this. Thus, by delving into gossip, the *Nefesh* is making a sophisticated attempt to divert focus from our own lives and our own faults to the lives and faults of others. It is a comfortable, convenient haven away from our own troubles and problems. And you know by now what I have to say about escaping from yourself and avoiding your own faults. It takes you right off the track of metaphysical health.

Of all the steps in this diet, for some people this may be one of the most radical. This week you will try to avoid as a pastime talking about other people's lives or shortcomings. You might find that with some of your friends and acquaintances you would have to redefine the way you converse over that espresso during lunch. This may take some getting used to.

There are, however, instances where divulgence of information about a third party is permitted, and sometimes mandated, for a constructive purpose.[5]

---

[4] Rabbi Yisroel Meir Hakohen Kagan, in The *Chofetz Chaim*, enumerates 31 commandments that are violated when speaking gossip and slander, called *Lashon Horah* in Hebrew.

[5] Thus, if what you are disclosing is necessary for a bride or groom to know about their future life partner, or is public knowledge that is repeated for the purpose of educating or benefiting society, then, depending on the manner in which the information is relayed, this would be permitted. The Jewish laws of appropriate speech are complex, and this is not intended as a full treatment of the subject.

The Truth about Lies

As pointed out in the previous chapter concerning the limitations of "anger geography," in the case of telling lies, too, the argument may surface that so long as nobody is being affected by the lie, what harm could there possibly be in lying? Similarly, here we would counter that even if nobody gets adversely affected by the lie the very mindset you assume when turning to lies has a detrimental affect on you. In order to achieve your ulterior motives, you are programming your mind to operate in a way that ignores your metaphysical health. As a result of your own decisions and actions, you can become numbed to your prior moral standards. Acting with integrity loses priority and you will have successfully blurred the line between truth and falsehood.

You're at a party and your intention is to impress everybody there with a thrilling story that happened to you. Not that thrilling in actuality, but if you delivered it raw and unenhanced it wouldn't draw as many oohs and aahs. So you add a few ingredients here and there, such as:

- You fell 12 feet to the ground instead of 6
- You only got 1 hour of sleep instead of 3
- You were unconscious for 2 hours instead of 35 minutes

So what? You may ask. Must I be so critical? So you embellished the story a bit to get extra attention. Nobody got hurt. *You* did. What happens typically is that based on its favorable reception the first time, you repeat the story at the next party. And then you repeat it countless times after that until—you cannot remember now exactly what did happen. It is possible to drum something into memory that didn't really happen at all, yet because of its repeated expression it has become a part of your "history." The line is blurred now between the actual truth and your fabrication. Programming one's mind this way can be unhealthy and even dangerous.

It's not that it starts out dangerous. Part of the sophistication of the *Nefesh* is that it advertises a little slip here and a little slip there as nothing to get all excited about. So you've repeated the half-truths until you're unsure now about the reality. Again, so what? Well, your slightly desensitized approach to the definition of honesty might be compared to a fissure that widens under increased pressure until, before you know it, the concept of honesty is a diluted and confused variable tainted by your agendas and philosophies. And you're even surprised how you got there.

When Dr Hwang Woo-suk and his research team from Seoul National University claimed to have cloned human embryonic stem cells, it naturally stunned the scientific world. He rose to international fame. Korea was exceedingly proud of him. Korean Air gave him and his wife free-first class tickets for a decade. Equally stunning was the revelation almost two years later that he had faked his results. His report was based on fabricated data.

What's interesting to note here is that this claim was not made by an amateur, a deranged individual who knew nothing about cloning or even science, seeking attention. Dr. Hwang had a PhD in Theriogenology and had successfully created the world's first cloned dog. This act was uncontested. It is possible that he believed that his confidence in his ability to clone the cells justified his claim, even if he hadn't done it just quite yet. It's possible that he believed it was only a matter of time before his efforts would prove genuine. Meanwhile, there were some tremendous personal advantages, relating to prestige, to taking the credit for it prematurely. The extent to which he had neatly tailored his own system of truth and integrity is illustrated in an interview conducted by BBC News,[6] several months before his fabrications were exposed. Asked if he had any regrets, he remarked, "I have no regrets. If I was born again I would want to follow the same way of life. I would want to do it all again and become the same person I am now. I am very proud of my scientific work not only for myself but also for all the people that it could help. All of mankind."

One gets the impression that this was or is his sincere belief. This is the ultimate goal of the *Nefesh* in its seemingly innocuous green light to a slightly sloping slippery road. One finds oneself in an alien belief system where everything one does continues to make sense.

Admittedly this is more of an extreme case of self-deception. We are not about to explore the real extremes such as pathological lying or mythomania. We will remain with the common-or-garden half-truths of which we convince ourselves, which are nevertheless detractors to clarity and to metaphysical health.

To this end, the Torah cautions,[7] *Distance yourself from a false word.* This is the source for the prohibition of lying.[8] Distance yourself from it. No other command in the Torah is expressed in this unusual manner, alluding to the extent to which falsehood can unwittingly lure individuals to their downfall.

Fill-in:

This is where you fill in your personal areas of challenge relating to speech on The Satellite Map. They are the "Inclusions" we spoke of in the last chapter. The following are examples or ideas for Inclusions that you could use or build on if you relate to them:

- I indulge too much in sarcasm
- My speech is a lot of hype and little content
- I'm always criticizing, but never complimenting
- I tell myself that the extra money I draw from the business is really owed to me because I work so hard
- I enjoy speaking about our crazy co-worker every time I get together with my friends after work

---

[6] Monday, 8 August, 2005.

[7] Exodus, 23:7.

[8] As pointed out by the *Pele Yoetz,* Rabbi Eliezer Papo, 1785–1826. The ninth of the Ten Commandments is actually a specific reference to not bearing false witness.

For our sample chart that follows, I selected two Inclusions from the above list: *I'm always criticizing, but never complimenting*, and *I tell myself that the extra money I draw from the business is really owed to me because I work so hard*, and filled in the chart based on these two challenges.

Try to fit whatever your Inclusions are into the following sub-categories, actually a digest of what we uncovered in this chapter:

- **Indiscriminate and Meaningless Speech:** Saying things out of hand because of little regard for the potency of speech.
- **Sarcasm:** Accumulated playful jabs can end up being harmful.
- **Gossip and Slander:** An invasion of privacy that is a dark and disorienting pleasure.
- **Lies:** Slight digressions from truth are the beginning of a slippery slope.

Those sub-categories that are highlighted in bold (which you can circle in red ink) are the Nerve Centers, your most profound areas of challenge. The two Inclusions in this sample belong to those Nerve Centers.

Umbrella 3: Speech Control

SUBCATEGORIES		**Indiscriminate and Meaningless Speech** Sarcasm Gossip and Slander **Lies**
INCLUSIONS	SUCCESS?	I'm always criticizing, but never complimenting. I tell myself that the extra money I draw from the business is really owed to me because I work so hard.
DAY 1 OBSERVATIONS	✔ ✘	I only noticed today how much I just let loose my criticism without second thought. It still didn't stop me from doing it, though.
DAY 2 OBSERVATIONS	✘	It's so hard to reverse an attitude of "the company owes me." I used the company credit card today for lunch with my wife.
DAY 3 OBSERVATIONS	✔ ✔	I actually resisted calling in "sick" so that I could go to the game. AND I didn't watch it on TV on company time, either.
DAY 4 OBSERVATIONS	✘ ✘	Whipped out the company card to pay for gas for my brother's car, and then had words for my boss who questioned where I'd been.
DAY 5 OBSERVATIONS	✘	Had nothing but criticism for my kids today.
DAY 6 OBSERVATIONS	✔ ✔ ✔	A co-worker ran an errand for me. When she returned, I made a conscious effort to thank her properly. Beforehand I found this difficult to do (I kind of expected it if she were a real friend). Then when I found out she had omitted a detail, I didn't say anything. When she walked away, I didn't even mumble under my breath.
DAY 7 OBSERVATIONS	✘	Since the company had ordered more than enough binders for its employees, I just took a few home with me. Who would miss them?

10

Step 7: The Giving Factor

The JFK Principle

IN HIS INAUGURAL ADDRESS ON JANUARY 20TH, 1961, PRESIDENT JOHN F. KENNEDY presented his country with a line that became etched into the national conscience: "Ask not what your country can do for you—ask what you can do for your country." The message of his speech in general was one of hope and inspiration for what lay ahead. If one were to look beyond the poetry and symmetry of his words, beyond the urgency and passion of his delivery, focusing instead on the meaning of the words themselves, one would be scrambling for the instruction sheet. Eh… practically, what does it mean, "ask not what your country can do for you—ask what you can do for your country"?

Of course it was not Kennedy's intention to give a nuts-and-bolts breakdown of the idea. In keeping with all other inspirational addresses, his approach was more literary than literal, employing the power of metaphor to reach the heart of the people. People understood from his words the general notion of self-sacrifice for one's country in a way that moved them, and in that sense the words achieved their purpose. But scrutinizing his message we'd realize just how demanding such a request is—nearly a complete reversal of the attitude our commercial society embraces and promotes. In effect the message tells you to stop thinking about your own needs and focus mainly on the needs of another entity. You are not merely being asked to sprinkle your self-absorbed day with tiny intervals of altruism. No, you are being asked to reverse your approach altogether with perhaps only a small allowance to sprinkle your altruism with tiny intervals of self-absorption. It says "No" to the giant finger pointed at your self-image from the freeway billboards, from the books promising you the world if only you would seize the moment, from the ads for cars that have nothing to do with cars but everything to do with the fuel-injected personality that supposedly will possess you as soon as you buy one. Kennedy's request is a dramatic shift away from the self. Taken seriously, it is a sudden call to sheer, unshakable devotion to the country that hosts you. And not when it suits you, but all the time.

There's no reason that this principle should apply to country alone. Anyone or anything in your life worth your utmost respect should also require the same level of devotion. The question is, why? Why would I dedicate myself entirely to a cause outside of myself? I can understand showing appreciation for those things. I am very grateful for the freedom my country offers me, for the support my spouse gives me, for the health of my family and friends. But does that mean I am now so indebted that I should be focused solely on what I should give and not what I should receive? There is a leap here I am not sure I am willing to take. The truth is, without a specific end goal in mind, without an understanding of the mechanics of giving, it would be extremely difficult to just become a giving machine. There would be little motivation to suddenly switch into "giving" overdrive unless I knew where this was taking me; unless I felt that I was reducing my focus on my self because the process of refocus itself was profoundly good for me.

Metaphysical health has always been our overarching goal. It is a goal consistent with all the steps of The Soul Diet, where all of our mini-goals meet; it is the ultimate and worthwhile ideal worth working for. It happens to be that giving is a very useful tool in restoring and maintaining metaphysical health; not least, as we will explain, it eliminates the confusion brought about by self-absorption.

Magical Mechanics

Rabbi Dessler[1] provides an illuminating insight into the mechanics of giving. A common misconception, promoted by our current culture, is that giving comes after love. Once you love someone, you will want to give to them. But first love has to be established. Rabbi Dessler tells us that the reverse is true: First you give, then you love.

What are we saying here? Firstly, realistically, we are going to acknowledge that humans are essentially selfish, not necessarily in a derogatory sense but in the sense of self-preservation. We are always looking out for ourselves, and what a good thing that is! Because if we wouldn't, who would? Self-preservation is thus really a positive trait preprogrammed in us for our own survival. There is nothing abnormal about immediately reserving a chunk of love for ourselves. This is healthy and helps us cope in the world; thus when we give of ourselves to another person we are taking that natural love we have for ourselves and planting it in the other person. We then see part of ourselves in that person, and begin to love that other person because part of us is inside them! The same is true of a cause to which we devote ourselves. Even if we didn't relate too well to the cause initially, by investing our energy and time in the cause the result is that we grow much closer to it because increasingly we see more of ourselves in that cause. Without denying our self-centered instincts, a relationship is being fostered through the mechanics of giving. Thus it is these very same self-preservation instincts that enable us to form the bond.

A striking example of how this concept manifests itself in relationships can be found in contrasting the love parents have for their children with the love children have for their parents. It is common for parents to love their children more than children love their parents. This is easy

---

[1] In *Michtav M'Eliyahu* Vol 11, pg 36.

to understand according to our reasoning. From the moment a child is conceived until well into adulthood parents fret over their every need. In fact, many parents give so much of themselves to their children that they spend more energy on their children then they do on themselves. Thus it is not difficult to understand how they love their children more than they love themselves. Much of who they are can be found invested in their children. (This also includes, for some of us, cases of unhealthy projection of our unfulfilled dreams onto our children.)

On the other hand, from the moment a child is conceived, the child begins to receive from its parents, and it is pretty much a one-way relationship until way into adulthood. Children see only a small part of themselves in their parents. For sure, under healthy conditions there is love and respect, but it generally does not compare to the feelings the parent has for the child.

Often, when parents get older and become more dependent on their children, the roles become somewhat reversed; and so do the feelings. The child may spend a great deal of energy taking care of his or her parents and in turn start to appreciate aspects about the parents that somehow had never been noticed before; and from this new perspective, the bond becomes stronger. These are the almost magical mechanics of giving, and are aptly reflected in a verse we quoted earlier in the chapter on anger:

"You shall love your fellow as yourself." As the meticulous inspector I have encouraged you to be, you should be raising your hand in objection. Why not just say, "You should love your fellow"? Why add *as yourself*? The answer should now follow easily. You have a natural love for yourself. When you give to others you will love others as yourself, literally. Your "self" is in others.

This is a wonderful principle to apply in many different situations. Let's say that you have a co-worker who drives you nuts. For some reason, you find everything about this person intolerable. You have spoken with your supervisor about transferring to a different workstation, but to no avail. How do you deal with this person? Your first thought might be to avoid this person as much as possible, not to engage him or her in conversation unless absolutely necessary. This might work, depending on the freedom you have to work separately. However, the most effective solution is also the most surprising: start giving to this other person. You may have to grit your teeth, but offer your help, bring things, even run errands for this individual. Your gritting might conceivably become growling, but watch the shift in your perspective as you start to soften on your opinion of the person. "Hey, you know," you tell yourself. "He's not as bad as I thought." Your own energy is valuable to you. When you are using it on people, it becomes valuable too.

In summary, the JFK Principle might be realistically achieved through an understanding of the mechanics of giving. You do not have to jump to a level of complete self-negation; rather you could spread yourself into the desired area by giving first and thus letting your connection develop naturally. Give first, then comes the connection. Surprise! Instead of completely nullifying yourself, you have spread yourself out.

Self-absorption occurs when you fail to spread yourself out, when you do not invest yourself in the right person or cause. If you expect a new state of giving to occur once love happens, you will be waiting for a very long time. You will be confused and frustrated by your experiences of what you think is love. A claim of love that does not result from giving is not likely to be genuine. More likely it falls into the realm of infatuation. "Love at first sight" is an adrenaline rush comprised of a bunch of sensory receptors beeping at full alert. You are receiving something, but many people are disappointed when, after a while, the adrenaline fades and the sensory receptors dull. They are not *receiving* anymore; it seems as though the love is fading. In truth, love never did exist. To generate love, you don't receive. You give. No adrenaline. No sensory receptors on full alert. You just give.

This week you will concentrate on giving of yourself to people and causes that are good for others and good for you, so that you may form a meaningful connection to them. You will try to rid yourself of the confusion of self-absorption by deciding to give, to extend yourself beyond the space that you occupy.

Look at me give

Nothing is simple, especially in this book. You would think that once you have the license to give, you can speed ahead at full throttle spreading yourself without concern all over the place. Technically, in a perfect world, that would be magnanimous of you. But in reality, the *Nefesh* is not about to be left behind in a dust cloud just because you have embarked on a visionary mission. The *Nefesh* will call an emergency planning meeting of all its agents to restrategize accordingly.

Somewhere along the route to your new altruistic goals, you begin hearing a voice. It's not a frightening voice, especially since the voice is yours. It starts to congratulate you for your achievements, to marvel at your noble purpose, your convictions for a better society and peace for all. There's no doubt about it—you enjoy what you are hearing. This voice begins to echo frequently and you think, *how right this voice is.*

I remember seeing a volunteer for a worthwhile cause being interviewed on the news several years ago. When asked about the work involved and its purpose, I noticed how she talked almost exclusively about herself: how she has always wanted to be involved in this, how she feels fulfilled in her work, how important she feels it is for others to be involved, how hard it was for her to make the choice of doing this work instead of doing other things, how she has always wanted to contribute someway and now she is so glad that this opportunity has come her way....

Not everybody is so inclined, but you have to watch out for the *Nefesh*'s reworked strategy here, which ironically uses your good deeds as a means to crown your ego, thus shrewdly re-routing your initially selfless efforts back to your self-image. Darn, you might say. If this *Nefesh* was a real-life lawyer, he'd be a multi-millionaire. Granted, most of the time it's better to give with improper motivations than not to give at all. But that's only from the perspective of the recipient. From the perspective of you, the giver's metaphysical health, you have an unhealthy obsession with your "selflessness."

Very often this conflict of interest comes to the fore where committees are involved, where multi-tiered bureaucracies are established to achieve common goals. Unfortunately these organizations are not free of politics, bickering, and, most notably, self-interest. An unhealthy ambition to top other performers might involve the same callous, hard-nosed tactics common in the corporate environment. Not infrequently one delights in seeing his or her name in lights, on executive boards, at the forefront of charitable drives. This is seemingly a forgivable fantasy yet often robs one of the original, more genuine motivation for reaching out. The appearance of one's face and name on a magazine cover featuring their city's Top 100 Movers and Shakers might be the fulfillment of one's ultimate dream. Meanwhile the worthy cause, the actual subject of what this individual has moved and shaken, takes a distant second place. In some ways, at least, it is difficult to fool oneself; and thus the likelihood is that the realization of one's misplaced priorities will soon enough dilute any real pleasure that comes from meaningful accomplishment.

Giving should remain an uncluttered, unsophisticated act of benevolence. In Jewish Law, the highest form of charity is that which is given anonymously. Your goal of metaphysical health mandates a certain level of humility. It's so easy to get side-tracked by unhealthy motivations and agendas, and humility is needed in order to think clearly, to remember your priorities. Otherwise your mind starts to fill with inflated ideas that take you places where you shouldn't go.

The Give and Take of Taking

Free market enterprise, or some percentage of it, is the celebrated dynamo behind most modern economies. An integral part of this system is: taking. If there would be no takers there would be no givers and the market would collapse. Entrepreneurs are constantly on the lookout for an untapped niche, essentially a group of not-yet satisfied takers. And businesses are created purely with those takers in mind.

One would reasonably assume that in social circles and in the privacy of your own home becoming a giver and not a taker is fine and dandy, but when it comes to business—well, come on, business is business. If I don't take profit, how am I going to pay the rent? Rabbi Dessler again discusses how to integrate the notion of giving in the business world. You might be inclined to furnish me with examples of corporate involvement in charity and humanitarian causes through sponsorships and (well-publicized) donations, but, alas, much of that has nothing other than keeping the company's bottom line in mind. I am referring rather to how the concept of giving might apply to the every-day goings on in a business. To understand this, it is necessary to dismantle our motivation for going to work in the first place.

Why do we work? (I know, I know. Try not to sigh. You will see it's worth it). The simplest response is actually the most commendable. I work because I have to. The work itself is not who I am, it's not the ultimate pursuit that underscores my entire existence. I work to live, not live to work. This may be the simplest answer but it's not necessarily the most common. The mere mention today of the word "career" has connotations of life-altering proportions. It means much more than the work you do. It's the direction you've taken. The culture you've adopted. It's what you're doing with your life. It's your investment in your future, especially after you've accumulated hundreds of thousands of dollars in student loans in pursuit of this grand personal design. Career guidance counselors, whose very existence draws from this phenomenon, will tell you that if you really want to achieve success in your field you have to live the dream: thus if you want to excel in medicine, you must read up in your spare time on the latest innovations in medicine. If you want to excel in law, you must keep up with legal news. You must spend as much spare time as you possibly can immersed in your field so that you can stay ahead of the game.

And then the employers will talk about employee loyalty. Hmmm, that doesn't just mean you shouldn't pocket the printer paper from the company copier for your own use. It means thinking about the company even when you're not on company time. The sweet-sounding incentive programs are there to encourage workers to dedicate themselves to company goals, "thinking beyond" the 9–5 strictures, so that their minds are fine-tuned to management objectives. There would be no need for policing employees if the employees themselves had personal goals so intimately in line with corporate ones that they had hardly any "self" left. This is a great business strategy, but it is a terrible life strategy!

Such curious "loyalty" is yet another cause of clutter—that which distracts you from remembering what's really important in your life. Just as the media seems conspired to drown you with sensory stimulation, inviting you to mold your life according to a Hawaiian timeshare pipedream, so, too, the business moguls who produce the business models seem to have conspired to drown you with far-reaching career options, each one inviting you to mold your life according to a lucrative partner-with-us pipedream. In reality such a narrow perspective on what counts in life causes only confusion and distortion of values. For proof, all you need do is ask the spouse or child of a Manhattan lawyer.

The healthiest approach to working is one that views a career as a means to put bread on the table. Now you have the time and ability to focus on family and personal growth. Most significantly, because your work is a means to an end, it becomes important because it helps you achieve your primary goals. Without the bread on the table, you cannot even begin to work on these goals. In that sense, the type of work you choose could be compared to the type of car you buy. For some people the driving experience is all-important. Style, color, torque, cabin noise are closely examined. For other people, all they want is to get from A to B. For the latter group, the car is important, but only because it enables them to get to their destination. Similarly, those who view their work as essentially a means of getting to their destination have a healthy outlook.

Now what does this mean for you? Well, if you work in one of those comfortable flexi-hour switch-my-work-mind-on, switch-my-work-mind-off jobs, and you chose it precisely because you could concentrate on what's important, then, good for you! Keep up the good work. But what if you work on the all-consuming corporate fast track which makes no stops for silly things like family? It's taking you close to a year to read this book because you read it between your non-booked hours of 3–4 in the morning. Well, I am not going to go so far as to tell you to quit this job. I do have a heart. Right, you say.

As stressed as your life is now, to suddenly drop everything and change would be even more stressful. So what can you do to mitigate the stifling effects of the corporate lifestyle? Well, you could play your part as the entrenched yes-person, yet on the inside begin to change the way you view your work. This is not as difficult as it sounds. In fact, because your new-found perspective provides you with a healthier direction, you will be happier with yourself. And anyone who is happier inside becomes more resolute about one's work. Not least, once the work is understood as a means to a noble end, it has meaning.

Practically, this could entail deciding to swing your bonus the way of a charity instead of your burgeoning stock portfolio. After all, you've redefined your purpose, and thus your motivation, for accumulating more than you need. Instead of grabbing a sandwich from the corner deli for your lunch you could arrange to meet your spouse/child/parent somewhere for a bite, even if it's only for fifteen minutes. It shows what's on your mind. And if you're not married or sharing a life because you've got no time for that—well...we need to talk. But let's leave it at that. And of course you could also use the workplace as an opportunity to focus on all the umbrellas of our ledger—from organizing your desk to learning to deal with impossible co-workers. There are ways of doing it, if you want to do it.

With this in mind, we can return to the question of how to relate to the concept of taking, a central feature of free market enterprise. When you approach your work as the means to an end your focus is less on what you can get out of it, and more on what you can contribute. Even when you are taking, you are doing it in order to give. Yes, taking is essential in the business world, but the reason for your taking is no longer self-absorbed. You view it as a means to much more principled goals. If it happens that you do strike oil in an untapped market, for example, you are cordially invited to collect your wealth like a carpenter collects his tools. The real work of what you are going to do with your takings, however, lies ahead of you.

Fill-in:

This is where you fill in your personal areas of challenge relating to giving on The Satellite Map. They are the "Inclusions" we spoke of in the last chapter. The following are examples or ideas for Inclusions that you could use or build on if you relate to them:

- I offer my help only if it doesn't inconvenience me, or only if it gets me somewhere too.
- I look at relationships as the way the other person makes me feel or what I can get out of that person.
- I get upset if I don't get thanked enough for the charity work or general good that I do.
- I am obsessed with getting the most out of my career, at the expense of getting or staying married or spending time with my family.
- I will only give money if I see it as an investment that will yield me a strong return.

For our sample chart below, I selected two Inclusions from the above list: *I look at relationships as the way the other person makes me feel or what I can get out of that person*, and *I am obsessed with getting the most out of my career, at the expense of getting married or spending time with my family*, and filled in the chart based on these two challenges.

Try to fit whatever your Inclusions are into the following sub-categories; which are really a digest of what we uncovered in this chapter:

- **Waiting to Receive:** Viewing giving as a consequence of affection, rather than an implementable tool for attaining affection
- **Self-Indulgent Giving:** Allowing the focus to turn inward on the giver's achievements.
- **Career Immersion:** Living to work rather than working to live
- **Pure Taking:** Viewing all money from the "bottom line" perspective rather than as a possible means to doing good.

Those sub-categories that are highlighted in bold (which you can circle in red ink) are the Nerve Centers, your most profound areas of challenge. The two Inclusions in this sample belong to those Nerve Centers.

Umbrella 4: The Giving Factor

SUBCATEGORIES		**Waiting to Receive** Self-Indulgent Giving **Career Immersion** Pure Taking
INCLUSIONS	SUCCESS?	I look at relationships as the way the other person makes me feel or what I can get out of that person. I am obsessed with getting the most out of my career, at the expense of getting married or spending time with my family.
DAY 1 OBSERVATIONS	✔ ✘	I decided to make my husband a special meal for dinner. But then while I was making the dinner I fixated about why he hasn't done something special for me in a long time, either.
DAY 2 OBSERVATIONS	✘	I had to cancel my daughter's birthday party because a major client needed an emergency meeting with me. I know my cancellation was wrong.
DAY 3 OBSERVATIONS	✔ ✔	I worked up the courage to cancel a different meeting to make the party. Although risking a possible backlash from the client, I realized that my daughter only has one childhood with me. I spent time with her at the party rather than making sure she had her friends and her gifts so that I could disappear to make phone calls.
DAY 4 OBSERVATIONS	✘ ✘	I played this mind game where I waited to see what my husband would get me for our anniversary before I did any reciprocal shopping. And when I saw that he didn't spend that much, neither did I.
DAY 5 OBSERVATIONS	✘	I was thinking today how my sister never calls me.
DAY 6 OBSERVATIONS	✔ ✔ ✔	I decided to call my sister, without thinking afterward that it was now her turn to call me. I then put it into my calendar to call her the following week.
DAY 7 OBSERVATIONS	✘	My husband didn't want me to apply for a particular promotion, and I had trouble fighting with my ambitious drive to get to the top.

11

Step 8: Intimacy

Vision From Outer Space

IF ALIENS WERE SENT ON A MISSION TO OBSERVE EARTHLING BEHAVIOR, no doubt many things would interest them and puzzle them. But nothing would cause them to scratch their antennae more than the earthling pursuit of sexual gratification. Observed from their vantage point, this process of hunting certain body parts for pleasure seems to defy explanation. Of course, reproduction is necessary for the propagation of the species, but why is it accompanied by an elaborate game of mind play? Why is it serviced by a multi-billion dollar trade industry, and an entire branch of literature ranging from the educational to what they call, for some reason, illicit or obscene. What on earth (or in outer space) does obscene mean anyway? Isn't this act natural? Why isn't the act of eating a sandwich obscene? Or reading a book, or changing a tire? Or washing the dishes? It's all mechanical, isn't it?

Why do these earthlings fantasize about this and not about taking out the garbage? Both are human responsibilities! While we will leave the aliens to resolve their quandary, it might do us well to at least put ourselves in a quandary. We tend to take all of this for granted, rarely going right to the root of these impulses raging inside of us. Instead we assume immediately that hunting body parts for pleasure is part of the package of being human, and so when we experience confusion in this area we work only with the facts as they are presented us—mainly topical treatment for a subject so immensely profound and mysterious. Even a therapist would deal with the sexual drive only as it manifests itself in relationships, interpreting and classifying individual behavior patterns according to known theories of causation. But it's doubtful a therapist would indulge in philosophical speculation, diving right back to creation of the human being and ask, "Well, why do we not spend as much of our day fantasizing about taking out the garbage?"

The failure to at least question the source and purpose of these sexual impulses accounts for a level of confusion in this area perhaps more than in any other. Those *What's happening to me?* books greeting kids on the brink of puberty often have patronizing overtones to them, as if to say, "we adults who wrote this book have this whole sex thing squared away, so here you go, let's just calmly do a 'Birds and Bees 101' and you're on your way."

Machines did not write those books. Humans did, and so long as pulses are beating and minds are ticking, sexual desire will invariably continue to throw curveballs and put spanners in the works, long after puberty. Even as they wrote these books, the authors might have been troubled by certain sexual thoughts or issues they were experiencing personally at that time. Very many adults, even those of ripe old age, are still befuddled by where this drive leads them, how it sometimes gets them into trouble and why it occupies such a huge chunk of their thought patterns; something particularly true of men.

The Ladies Home Journal[1] reported that men think about sex very frequently, sometimes several times an hour. And yet, from a legal standpoint, when the clock strikes twelve on the eve of our eighteenth birthdays, something magical is supposed to happen. While we might not be expected to turn into pumpkins, we are expected to turn into mature people capable of weathering exposure to indecent material with minimal fallout. A day earlier we were deemed vulnerable and corruptible, and a day later we are deemed "safe"? Of course *nobody* qualifies from the school of sexual desire, simply because life is that school, and the only way to qualify, really, is to not have life anymore. Merely accepting these desires as natural and then working from there, misses the point. In order to treat the specific problems associated with the intimate experience we need to understand these issues in greater depth.

The Power of Intimacy

When referring to the physical relations of Adam and Eve in the conception of Cain and Abel, the Torah uses a seemingly strange term: "The man had *known* his wife."[2] What does it mean that he knew her? Of course he knew her—she was his wife! The deliberate usage of the word, "know" to describe the physical act goes beyond an attempt to be euphemistic. It reflects an entire paradigm of the Torah's approach to marital relations. There are three general levels or categories comprising Jewish knowledge: The first is *Chochma*, or external wisdom. This is the knowledge acquired through study, the digestion of information that we store in our memory banks. It is knowledge that is superficial in the sense that we access it when we need it, but it does not become a part of us; it is as if we were retrieving information from a computerized data base. For example, studying the history of American economic development, or the science of photosynthesis in plants, broadens one's knowledge base of the world. Yet generally it does not penetrate the mind on a personal level so that you find yourself trying to apply Keynesian Fiscal Policy to how to treat your spouse, or so that you start thinking that Chlorophyll would be a great name for your newborn baby.

The second type of knowledge is called *Bina*, or insight, a more internalized level of understanding whereby you can take that existing knowledge you acquired through *Chochma* and apply it to various situations. In other words, it is no longer merely raw data collecting in your memory; you can process it intuitively so that you are able to make it do things for you. The knowledge

---

[1] Hank Herman, "Question: How Often Do Men Think About Sex? Answer: He's Probably Thinking About it Right Now," 110.3. 1993: 98.

[2] Genesis (4,1).

has become more personalized. For example, as a result of learning the effects of expansion and contraction, you realize you will have to account for that by leaving sufficient gaps between the bricks of your patio as you set them out. This is your own contribution to the knowledge you originally acquired. You took that knowledge and built on it. Fascinatingly, the Hebrew word for building is *boneh*, directly related to *binah*, insight.[3]

The third level of knowledge is one that fuses the knowledge with the self. It is the most intimate form of knowledge and is known as *Daas*, knowledge that you have made so close to you that it is inseparable from your personality. For example, if someone asks you for your mother's name you do not have to put them on hold while you work out that information. "Well, let's see. My father's name is Donald and he got married in 1963, and if I remember correctly, it was to a woman named...." No, you don't have to go through that process. You don't even have to think for a nanosecond before you respond. The knowledge is so intrinsic it is as real and accessible as your right hand.

When the verse speaks of Adam "knowing" his wife, this third level of knowledge is represented in the language. This means that the physical experience was the deepest expression of intimate knowledge possible between man and woman. If your mother's name is like your right hand, then this experience allows your spouse to be as integral to you as your right hand. However, this type of intense intimacy is achieved only if this is your very intention when together. If you have only base intentions—you just happen to be satisfying your desires through your spouse—then the experience falls way short of that level of intimacy. You can hardly be considered "knowing" each other if the act amounts to nothing more than two people using each other for need gratification. In fact, when people speak about being "unsatisfied" in the bedroom, it is often because there is actually too much focus on sexual gratification and too little focus on the intimacy it should generate. You can never be satisfied if your focus is chiefly on satisfying your physical desires. It's an asymptote: your desires never quite reaching the X-axis.

This is another very serious wound inflicted on the Western psyche by the media. The implication of any screen romance is that true intimacy is only possible when your life takes on the dimensions of a Hollywood studio. Sizzling passion and mood-perfect music set the passing grade for classification as a decent relationship, and many lifetime viewers struggle with a deluded sense of inadequacy because they think they are failing to meet the grade, as we witnessed with the woman watching Charley and Vera's moonlit dinner in Chapter Four. A real sense of intimacy involves an entirely different focus, an intent to "know" each other as did the first man and his wife. With this in mind, we can begin to understand the origin and purpose behind these impulses. They are catalysts to that very powerful level of intimacy, if used properly. With these impulses, the body is preparing itself for a profound connection with another human being.

---

[3] The two words share the same grammatical root of ב נ ה

The alien who began asking all those questions would receive the following response, based on what we've now learned:

You're right that physical relations would be a purely mechanical act if all it set out to achieve was mechanical need gratification. Then it would make no sense that these cravings occupy our minds so much more than the craving for taking out the garbage (does anybody in their right mind crave such a thing?). But the truth is that's *not* all it sets out to achieve. The deeper purpose behind physical relations is an intense level of intimacy with another person, thereby requiring a craving commensurate with that intensity. Only profoundly intense desires can facilitate that level of profound intimacy. As a result, you have a very solid bond, so much so that the Torah describes the intended union of Adam and Eve as "and they shall be as one flesh."[4] His right hand is her right hand. In fact, if you follow the entire build-up to this point in the Torah, you will note that initially, before woman was created, the verse tells us, "in the image of God He created *him*; male and female He created *them*."[5] Who is *them*? Woman has not been created yet! From this the sources[6] derive that man was hermaphroditic, possessing both male and female reproductive organs, and then Eve was separated from Adam. So when Adam and Eve bond together later to become "one flesh," they are to some extent returning to their original state of oneness.

So where does confusion in this area come from? Confusion reigns when those profoundly intense desires are channeled toward a mechanical experience. Or you have no idea where to direct them. Or you have never ever heard of the concept of "knowing" your spouse, so how were you supposed to understand anything about this? In any event, confusion in this area has the potency to knock you off your track toward metaphysical health in a way that is so unnerving, so debilitating, and so startling that it would be worth it to write this book for this week's challenge alone.

As with any of the umbrellas of this soul diet, it will take a lot longer than a week to really gain some genuine advances in this area, but this is when you can at least begin to explore changing the way you think about physical relationships; that is how you gradually become tuned to the deeply-fulfilling power of intimacy as opposed to the self-centered pursuit of need gratification.

Today's Pornography is Tomorrow's Art

Intimacy can be compared to gold. Gold is a precious metal commanding a high purchase price. But what makes gold such a sought-after commodity? Is it the renowned glitter and sheen of its hue, and the impressive sturdiness of its weight? Well, these may be collaborating factors, but gold's primary value lies in its scarcity and degree of inaccessibility.

If gold were as common and accessible as sand on the beach—you could just scoop up gold particles with your hand and let them run through your fingers as you take your morning stroll—then its market value would drop as fast as gravity would allow. No one is paying $400 an ounce for

---

[4] Genesis (2, 24).

[5] Genesis (1,27).

[6] Bereishis Rabbah (8,1).

beach sand, no matter how soft or golden its texture. Similarly, intimacy derives its value from its inaccessibility to the public domain. Intimacy is, by definition, a very close, private bond—and if any of that intimacy becomes exposed to the public, it is no longer private and therefore no longer intimate. Its value plummets.

If a couple decides to flaunt their relationship in front of others through overt display of physical affection, the attention they're drawing from others may be massaging their egos, but it also happens to be eroding the intimacy between them. In fact, their experience is no longer intimate, because they are sharing it with the world. How generous of them. But sadly, when they arrive home and there is no one left to admire their sensual tapestry but themselves, their physical interaction feels diluted. There is a natural expectation that a feeling of specialness should exist between them once they're behind closed doors, a unique chemistry to which only they are privy. The problem is they have already exposed it to the world, so something definitely feels lacking between them now. To make matters worse, this is when the *Nefesh* jumps on the "I'm-not-getting-what-I-need-from-my-relationship bandwagon," and tells you that perhaps you made a mistake by even getting involved with this person. The magic is gone.

Well, of course the magic is gone. You poured it out like confetti over an open air stadium. It may very well have nothing to do with the actual person you chose. This problem extends to all areas of immodesty and indecency. A natural consequence of more and more exposed intimacy is that those areas of the body that once caused very potent stirrings upon being exposed, do not "do anything" for people anymore. Why? Because people see themselves as progressive and now regard what was once taboo as being beauty and art in its natural state. Sounds really wonderful. But it's really sad. What should have excited them if they were normal red-blooded individuals with acute sensitivity to the sexual impulse, doesn't do anything for them anymore. That's not progressive—that's dysfunctional.

When someone can pore over exposed physical images with nothing but an academic interest —noting the lighting, the contrast, the brilliance of the colors – one has to wonder how damaged their sensors are! The level of desensitization can be astounding. People can stroll those particular beaches where it's not just the beauty of the azure sea that is on display, and many of them won't even look twice. They claim they are getting in touch with nature. Would that not be losing touch with nature? Becoming numbed to the instincts you were born with is hardly something to be proud of.

Senator Dick Ackerman[7] notes the extent to which the legal definition of "obscene" has changed since the end of the 19th century. In 1897, the Supreme Court considered advertisements for "baths" and "massages" to be "obscene, lewd, lascivious, and indecent,"[8] and presumed such advertisements were a pretext for illicit sexual activity for compensation. Today even moral watchdog groups are

---

[7] A member of the California State Senate, in an article for *Nexus Journal,* "Technology and Obscenity: Ever-changing Legal Challenges," Volume 10, 2003. Chapman University School of Law: 37–47.

[8] Dunlop v. United States, 165 U.S. 486, 490 (1897) cited by *Nexus Journal.*

hardly likely to bat an eyelid. The definition of obscenity was amended in 1957, and again in 1973, when the court added the inevitable rule of exception that if the illicit work in question had any "redeeming literary, artistic, political or scientific value," it would not be legally prohibited.[9]

In retrospect, the 1897 court decision is likely to be viewed by many as prudish and backward, and the 1973 decision as enlightened and progressive. Yet, ironically, if the court of 1897 would be given a peek at today's standards, they would have nothing but pity for those for whom the line between pornography and art is blurred. It would be viewed as a disability that inhibits normal functioning. A healthy individual, they would propose, is one whose normal physiological reaction to provocative imagery is sharp and acute.

The way the current system operates, the law will have to continue to be amended as standards degenerate, when today's pornography becomes tomorrow's art. "Family" films, books and internet sites will continue to incorporate that which was previously considered inappropriate. And in this process, the real, precious value of intimacy will continue to drop to rock bottom levels, and the meaning of genuine intimacy will slowly become a thing of the past. Sigh. I sound a little pessimistic, I admit. But the truth is, an insight like this is meant to *inspire*, not depress you. "Oh. Come on," you protest. "How could all this commentary of doom possibly be considered inspiring?" Well, the thing is, when you read and process this information, you are immediately ahead of the game. As I mentioned previously, this area of our conscience can cause so much confusion and anxiety specifically because we don't analyze and study it enough.

Once we've opened up the portals of investigation to ascertain just what is intimacy, we've taken a giant step in detangling the mess. Basically, you could sum it up this way: *If you know what intimacy is not, you can work towards what intimacy is*. If you follow this week's challenge of restoring your sensitivity to intimacy, even if it's just the decision to do so, you may be reversing a very negative trend in your attitude toward relationships. Let's examine some of the practicalities:

The Subtleties – Nudge, Nudge, Wink, Wink

Please forgive me for gnawing away at accepted societal norms. I understand that I might be labeled for what I am about to say (and most probably for what I've said thus far) as one who dwells firmly in the camps of the conservative, the extreme, the fanatic, where right is always right and left is always wrong. While I will disagree with you about that, I can understand where you are coming from. After all, accepted norms are like old, hoary mountains. They are *there*. Any restrictions imposed on them are immediately considered ridiculous and fanatical. No further questions, your honor.

Thus you might find it disconcerting when I suggest that it's better for a couple to avoid having strong friendships with others of the opposite sex. A married woman should not have a strong

---

[9] Miller v. California, 413 U.S. 15, 36–37 (1973), cited by *Nexus Journal*.

friendship with another man, and a married man should not have a strong friendship with another woman. There, I dropped the bomb.

It's a subtle bomb, with fragments perceived only by the astute. I am referring to things more intricate than the *Harry Met Sally* phenomenon, which proposes that friendships inevitably lead to full-blown relationships. My focus is on the "It's Nothing" syndrome—the alleged ordinary conversations and ordinary time spent together with a member of the opposite sex that *don't* necessarily lead to romantic relationships. This is where it gets tricky.

Pam and her husband were at a party where all the guests were mingling, forming their own little conversation units around the house. A natural consequence was that people who arrived together didn't necessarily stay together as they were drawn in different directions depending on the people and conversations that interested them. Initially, this suited Pam just fine, as she spotted a friend of hers who had recently given birth, and she wanted to catch up with her and get all the news about the baby. So her husband was left to stroll the avenue of hors d'oeuvres and their multi-toothpicked options. This was when Carla, recently divorced, approached him to chat. Out of the corner of her eye, Pam noticed this. She shifted uncomfortably as she tried her best to listen to her friend's animated recounting of getting stuck in traffic on the way to the hospital.

She couldn't hear what Carla was saying—they were too far away. But she became unnerved by Carla's facial expressions, the gestures with her hands. And her husband, too, seemed to respond in kind, with gestures that Pam felt belonged exclusively to her—*You know, that special affectionate way he speaks with me.* And then Pam chided herself for being foolish. The details of her friend's labor experience now were passing right over her head as she tried to fight this feeling of… well, jealousy that had overcome her. After all, they were just having a normal conversation in public. How could she be reacting so childishly? This internal battle endured with no outcome until Pam was reunited with her husband later on. She figured she'd just ask the question casually. "So what were you and Carla talking about?" she asked as she swallowed an olive off a toothpick. Her husband glanced at her, searching her face. He had known her for too long to be fooled by the supposed nonchalance. A clear accusation was in the works here. "Insurance premiums," he answered her with a trace of irritation. She stopped chewing. "Really?" Her husband sighed. "Yes, really." He waited for a retreat. But she was still undecided. You can guess what happened after that. He felt accused. She felt misunderstood. If ever the conditions were ripe for a full-blown argument in the car on the way home, this was it.

At first glance, we would take Pam to task for being over-protective. We would tell her to relax and to give her husband the benefit of the doubt. It's really, really difficult to turn insurance premiums into evocative material. But we are also being naïve if we think that her feelings are unfounded. She herself may not be able to express it or fathom it, but the conversation her husband had with Carla contained various nuances that are indicative of a certain style men unwittingly employ when talking with women.

In many cases, men simply carry themselves differently in social conversations with women than they do with their male friends. With their male friends, heterosexual men tend not to be concerned about their posture, about presenting themselves in an endearing way, and most notably about smiling endlessly as they talked. A suave continuous smile as a man talks to a woman, even about insurance premiums, is almost a trademark of the subtleties of male-female interaction. In any event, these were some of the signals Pam was picking up, gestures that she believed belonged to her only. They were signals that she saw as an intrusion to the intimacy she had with her husband. This is not being over-protective. Although she could have handled it better, Pam was justified in trying to protect her special intimacy with her husband. She didn't want him to share it with anyone else. On some level she felt it tug at her security; that meant more than anything else in the world to her.

These are some of the practicalities involved in preserving and treasuring intimacy. They require an effort to avoid lengthy and involved social exchanges with members of the opposite sex: no private meetings for coffee, no "harmless" dancing together at weddings, no late night conversations "about nothing." (Late night is an especially vulnerable time to breaches in intimacy.) As I said, you may find my conservative approach disconcerting, but if you want to take steps to restore and maintain genuine and profound intimacy with your partner, that person will be the only focus of your affection. You will also resist the urge to put your relationship on public display for all to marvel at. If it makes you feel any better, you might want to think of it as preservative rather than conservative.

Fences are the Best Defense

What do you do with your horde of gold? Well, my guess is that you most probably don't leave it out on the front porch next to the gas lamp and the bag of fertilizer. You don't just tuck it neatly under your bed next to your slippers and your roller skates. You don't even keep it in your house at all. It's locked away behind monster metal doors in an underground bank vault. That's what you would call a preventative measure to ensure this precious metal remains in your hands, that it does not begin to slip through your fingers, causing a potentially devastating blow to your resources. Your stash of newspapers, on the other hand, is not carefully guarded at all. In fact it lies quite openly on the recycling mound close to the curb.

It all depends upon your approach. If intimacy for you is like gold, you'll savor and cherish it, and you'll recognize the need to protect it. If it's like yesterday's newspaper, you will continue to let its value bottom out and you will continue to wonder why your relationship is so drab. Intimacy is reactive, not proactive. If you make a determined effort to preserve it, intimacy is strong and intense; if you let it go, intimacy is diluted and unremarkable.

When you realize the value and the beauty of true intimacy, the one with which Adam "knew" Eve, it will only be natural that you would want to protect such a thing. You would set up "fences" towards that end. You would, for example:

— avoid gazing at certain features of others as they walk by, which up to now you have dismissed as harmless entertainment. It may appear harmless, but through this behavior you are nevertheless rerouting the drive reserved for your partner. It's worse, of course, when you're caught looking. Nobody says it out loud, but the partner's sentiment is quite palpable: *I rank second-best now, don't I?* Not at all healthy for intimacy. The walls of intimacy begin to crumble at the notion of a downgraded connection.

— Avoid dressing up with the specific intent of attracting or making an impression on members of the opposite sex. You may not even be conscious of it, but the selection of certain types of clothing (or the absence of certain clothing) may cause a natural chemical reaction in the eye of the beholder. This may sound like the Surgeon General's Warning, and perhaps that is how it would be formulated if society did indeed place as much value on preserving metaphysical health as it did physical, but it is important to realize that this code of dress is exactly that—a code. It communicates to the person with whom you're chatting that you'd like the conversation to be as open-minded as your style of dress. It can establish a rapport that works more off the steam from the chemical combustion taking place than the actual content of the conversation.

If we looked at it from a logical perspective, it would not make sense that we would deliberately risk the special intimacy we have with those we love merely for the momentary thrill of having someone else stare us up and down.

There will be those of you who will be taken aback by this. Who am I to tell you what to wear? This has gone too far. How could I be so backward and pedantic as to restrict your style of dress? It is a freedom to which you are entitled. It is a vehicle for expression of your persona. It is a celebration of the release from the shackles of old-fashioned oppression....

Yes, I know. If that is the way you feel then I am not going to try to talk you out of it. All I am going to say is that much of the "self-expression" ideology doesn't care about what the other person thinks. If the other person feels slighted by your outward gestures to the public, well that's too bad. The other person is expected to respect your self-expression. True, this may very well work smoothly for some couples. They may interact congenially and lead successful lives. But don't expect intimacy, at least our definition of it anyway. How could a feeling of utter devotion exist between two people when it is being spread thin amongst others?

— Avoid chat rooms, both real and virtual. The nuances of interchange are rarely innocuous, and as we see in the media chapter it could even lead to affairs, both on and off-line.

The general rule of thumb is that, if you are scrupulously honest with yourself, *you will know* when you are breaching the boundaries of intimacy. You will detect that extra sparkle in the conversation in the eyes of the person you're addressing, in the way you are holding yourself. This is a very difficult challenge (what's new?) But in this case, as difficult as it is to preserve intimacy, the reward is immeasurable. You will begin to notice almost right away a marked strengthening in your relationship and an unprecedented bond that you will begin to feel at your core. This is real intimacy.

Fill-in:

This is where you fill in your personal areas of challenge relating to intimacy on The Satellite Map. They are the "Inclusions" we spoke of in the last chapter.

The following are examples or ideas for Inclusions that you could use or build on if you relate to them:

- I like to dress provocatively
- I'm married but enjoy the excitement of flirting
- I look at the wrong type of imagery
- I don't find my marital relations satisfying
- My parents taught me that a normal person 'plays the field' before settling down. Now I find it hard to value commitment.

For our sample chart below, I selected two Inclusions from the above list: *I like to dress provocatively*, and *I'm married but enjoy the excitement of flirting*, and filled in the chart based on these two challenges.

Try to fit whatever your Inclusions are into the following sub-categories; they are really a digest of what we uncovered in this chapter:

- **Mechanical Relationship:** Rather than viewing the physical act as a deeper intimate connection, it is nothing more than a mechanical release of urges.
- **Desensitization:** Over-exposure to indecent imagery has caused less sensitivity to intimacy.
- **Attitude Towards Modesty:** A belief in exposing that which is intimate has eroded intimacy between partners.
- **Easily Trapped:** Vulnerability to the sexual impulse can quickly derail a person.

Those sub-categories that are highlighted in bold (which you can circle in red ink) are the Nerve Centers, your most profound areas of challenge. The two Inclusions in this sample belong to those Nerve Centers.

Umbrella 5: Intimacy

SUBCATEGORIES		Mechanical Relationship Desensitization **Attitude towards Modesty** **Easily Trapped**
INCLUSIONS	SUCCESS?	I like to dress provocatively. I'm married but enjoy the excitement of flirting.
DAY 1 OBSERVATIONS	✔ ✘	I tried to dress more conservatively when I went out with my husband but I still caught myself talking playfully with this other guy there.
DAY 2 OBSERVATIONS	✘	It was hot today, so I succumbed and used it as an opportunity to show off my new skimpy dress, and I enjoyed the stares I got.
DAY 3 OBSERVATIONS	✔ ✔	I chose to dress modestly and felt regal! Best of all my husband appreciated my reserving my intimacy for him only.
DAY 4 OBSERVATIONS	✘ ✘	A male co-worker wanted to take me for lunch to talk about his career. From the way he asked me, I should have known that his interest stretched beyond career counseling. And the thing is, I didn't resist it, and actually enjoyed the meeting, even though I knew that it encroached on the intimacy with my husband.
DAY 5 OBSERVATIONS	✘	Everybody else was dressed provocatively, so how could I possible stand out?
DAY 6 OBSERVATIONS	✔ ✔ ✔	Not only did I turn down an "innocent" coffee with a lonely male friend, but I invited him to dinner with me and my husband so that we could talk afterwards while my husband worked in the next room. Well, what do you know? He wasn't interested in that. I learned a lot today!
DAY 7 OBSERVATIONS	✘	The idea of buying a whole new "modest" wardrobe intimidates me.

12

Step 9: Goal Control

Worth the Wait

GOALS, GOALS, GOALS MIGHT BE CONSIDERED THE SELF-HELP VERSION of the real estate mantra: location, location, location. Thousands of books and workshops are dominated by this one word serving as the undisputed focus, and yet in this book we've hardly touched on the topic thus far.

There's a reason for that. Setting goals prematurely can be extremely detrimental to a person. The word is wrapped in very appealing packaging, luring unsuspecting innocents into a starry-eyed vision of personal utopia where allegedly nothing and nobody should stand in the path toward that achievement.

You may have heard the following urgent whispers in your ear:

- If you put your mind to it, you will achieve your dream.
- People with healthy self-esteem will end up succeeding (a sneaky one).
- Tell yourself, "I am going to win this" and you will.
- Only you are stopping yourself from reaching your goals.
- Don't listen to what others tell you. Just follow your heart (the worst one).

Am I taking issue with the accuracy of these statements? No. In fact, the Talmud testifies, "In the way that a person wants to go, God will lead him there."

So now it appears I have bolstered the above whispers with support from the Talmud. On closer inspection, you will realize that the Talmud is not telling you what to do, *it's merely reporting the reality*. Yes, the will of a person is extremely powerful, and God will lead people the way of their will, but that is true whether or not that way is good for the person.

Herein lies the key: It is so easy to launch oneself at a goal that promises untold self-satisfaction. And often we do so without ever stopping to think, Is this goal good for me? What I want is not necessarily what I need. Is this goal something that the people in my life who matter to me will embrace? Is this goal something that will involve compromising my time spent with them? Is this goal directly conflicting with any of the steps of The Soul Diet?

That's why most of the umbrellas came first. By working through each and every step in the preceding weeks, you have carved your direction towards metaphysical health. Even though you may have stumbled here and there, you are focused, you're on track. Now that you're etching your most profound challenges onto the paper in front of you, you are equipped to scrutinize the goals marketed to you by the gurus and to determine whether or not you should take them on, whether or not they will indeed compromise your overarching plan of metaphysical health.

Let's take a sample of personal resolutions and put them to The Soul Diet test. The various steps are referenced in parenthesis.

1. You have resolved to lose weight.
Questions you will now ask yourself:
   – How much time will this diet or exercise program take away from my family or other priorities? (**Order and Fitness**)
   – Am I going to obsess with this program and forget that dieting is a means, not an end? (**Order and Fitness**)
   – If someone I love disagrees with what I am doing or how I am doing it, how I am I going to react? (**Anger Control; Speech Control**)
   – Is there a possibility that I will develop a conceit about losing the weight and enjoy comparing myself to overweight people who just can't "get their act together" like I could. (**Speech control**)
   – Will I make every effort to accommodate the rest of my family's nutritional tastes, instead of expecting them to automatically conform to mine? (**Giving Factor**)
   – Is part of my motivation to become appealing to men women other than my husband/ wife? (**Intimacy**)

2. You have decided to go for a career in corporate law.
Questions you will want to ask yourself:
   – Is my vision of the daily life of a corporate lawyer realistic, or is it shaped by media-manufactured machinations? (**Media Fast**)
   – Will I have time to make sure I am eating well and getting sufficient sleep? (**Order and Fitness**)
   – Will I be able to speak with integrity and avoid unnecessary defamation of character? (**Speech Control**)
   – Will my job become my life? (**Giving Factor**)
   – Will my focus be the preservation of justice or a self-absorbed pursuit of power? (**Giving Factor**)

3. You want to be an Olympic athlete.

Questions you will want to ask yourself:

- Many athletes ask God to help them get on the team and win the gold. Have I considered that God might not want me to get involved in the first place in a pursuit that would radically affect my family and social life? (**Order and Fitness**)
- Will my body take a hammering to the extent that there is some level of impairment after I'm done with my career? (**Order and Fitness**)
- How do I handle those close to me who aren't as keen about my decision as I am? (**Anger Control; Speech Control**)
- How will I treat my competitors? (**Anger Control; Speech Control**)
- Is it possible that my desire for Olympic victory is a self-absorbed pursuit of power and control? (**The Giving Factor**)

4. You want to develop a "web presence" – setting up your own blog, joining chat rooms.

Questions you will want to ask yourself:

- How strong is my capacity to keep to a time limit? Will I get drawn into sitting for hours in front of the screen? (**Media Fast; Schedule Slimming**)
- Is it possible that I will develop more meaningful conversations with (sometimes anonymous) on-line contacts than I will with those with whom I live? (**Media Fast; Schedule Slimming**)
- Have I considered the dangers of being drawn into illicit on-line relationships? (**Media Fast; Intimacy**)
- The blog culture promotes frank, unrestrained expression, where the courtesies of cordial interchange are often deliberately dispensed with. Will constant engagement in this style of expression begin to affect the way I speak to people in general? (**Speech Control**)
- Am I aware that I am placing myself at greater risk of viewing indecent and obscene imagery and literature just by clicking on my browser? If I have my own blog, I will be so much more invested in being on-line much of the time, thus exponentially increasing this risk. (**Intimacy**)

5. You have decided to dedicate yourself to battling some form of world injustice.

Questions you may want to ask yourself:

- Have I done my homework? Have I performed a thorough examination of the facts, or did I let my adrenaline overtake me based on peripheral information fed to me by the media? (**Media Fast; Anger Control**)
- Is this a cause that takes priority over other important people or things in my life? (**Schedule Slimming; Order and Fitness**)
- Will I adopt an approach of ruthless condemnation of those who have a dissenting view,

or will I conduct myself with dignity, employing a more proactive style? (**Speech Control**)

- Will I be tempted to "adjust" the truth to suit my agenda, especially if I have gone and dedicated my life to the cause? (**Speech Control**)
- Am I using this mission as a means to self-actualization, rather than being passionate about the actual cause itself? (**Giving Factor**)

Asking all these questions at the outset should at the very least give you pause for reflection, delaying the launch of your new idea even as your engines are thundering beneath you, urging you to take off. It is when we fail to ask these questions that we sometimes find ourselves well downstream of the idea or goal; this is when we feel utterly dejected, wondering why it seems that although we worked hard to achieve that goal, and we succeeded, so many other problems cropped up "out of nowhere," making life miserable. Achieving that one goal was supposed to bring on utopia; but so many other challenges have not only banished utopia but ushered in desolation.

Perhaps it was Nirvana rather than utopia, but Kurt Cobain's life is perhaps an illustration of fame's unspoken byproduct seizing the helm and driving a person to self-destruction. In testing the correlation between fame and an increase in self-consciousness, Mark Schaller of the University of Columbia[1] notes that as Cobain's popularity increased, his lyrics indicated more of a focus on himself. The idea is that such acute inward focus could eventually lead to self-destruction.

Thus it is not a minor concern when I ask you about your intentions when you set yourself goals. In case you think that kind of thing only happens to celebrities and "fringe elements," all we would have to do is consider the outcome of ignoring the questions that need to be asked in the above examples, and we would realize the extent of the impact these factors have on our stability.

- It turns out that the dieter does achieve substantial weight loss, attracting myriad admiring looks and remarks. However she completely obsesses about her diet and is not particularly concerned about her husband's objection to it and now her marriage has a good-sized wedge in it.

- The young lawyer is raking in the cash and sailing on the prestige of his first class flying privileges, but he does indeed find that he is unable to have any life outside the paper-flooded office he inhabits. He is physically and mentally drained, and yearns in vain to have a normal family life.

- The athlete's tears of joy drip onto the gold medal she is sporting. She has achieved the dream, except that her personal life is a nightmare because nobody, absolutely nobody, is capable of being understanding of her schedule.

---

[1] Department of Psychology, University of British Columbia, Vancouver, BC, Canada V6T 1Z4 in an article entitled, "The Psychological Consequences of Fame: Three Tests of the Self-Consciousness Hypothesis," *Journal of Personality* 65:2, June 1997: 291–309.

– The new blogger is wildly successful, with thousands of new and regular visitors per day, but he finds he rarely has time for (and interest in) conversing normally with people off-line, and has retreated into a peculiar, private cyberworld.

– The activist has made tremendous strides in her protests and lobbying, achieving several concessions from the offending organization. She also finds that, because of her indignation, she has become short-tempered and seems to snap at every opportunity. As a result, she and her husband are in counseling now.

I hope that by now you have really begun to see how this book comes together, unifying all the elements into one package. Metaphysical health is achieved only through rigorous scrutiny of our personalities, our choice of lifestyle, and our selection of goals.

Mental Cardiology

You may also have begun to see evidence of what we proposed back in Chapter two, that unbridled worship of the rhythms of the heart is not the way to go about setting your goals, if you know what's really good for you. We explained that it doesn't mean blocking the heart; rather, we should let rational thought and objectivity determine where and how to direct the heart.

The Talmud teaches, *A person should study that which his heart desires*. And in describing how people choose their career, *Rashi*[2] writes that even the most unappealing job in the world[3] has a person who eyes it as his or her choice. Basically, someone's heart will desire this type of work, regardless of its drawbacks. Evidently the messages of the heart are indeed important. Motivational speakers will, of course, push this point home several times. But what we are stressing is that those messages have to be immediately put under a microscope before you can go any further. If they are then approved, you do not only have approval from your emotions you also have it from your intellect. This type of synthesis is very powerful—you are achieving your goals without compromising your metaphysical health. In fact, you are strengthening your metaphysical health. So whether you are choosing your career, choosing your life partner, or choosing how to make your mark on the world, this synthesis of the heart and mind is vital in making sure you stay healthy.

Set the Goals

Spend this week thinking about the goals you have/want to set your for yourself, specifically whether they compromise the standards you yourself have set in the charts you filled in for each step of The Soul Diet.

Like the other steps, you may not be able to do this in one week. But you could make a start. Discuss your goals with others for their feedback, especially with those close to you. After all, they

---

[2] See footnote § 9. Here he comments on Talmud Brachos 43b.

[3] Such as the tanning of skins, apparently a foul-smelling, messy task.

will be the ones most likely to bear the brunt of any drawbacks associated with the attainment of the goal. The most fundamental move you're making is the willingness to accommodate the thoughts of others—it is so contrary to the single-minded focus inside all those achiever books. You're not simply asking others for their starred review of your ideas, you're actually bracing for a possible change in plans depending on how they react—because these people might just mean more to you than your own self-centered fantasies.

Follow-through

One of the consequences of the invasion of imagery, philosophies and hype in our every day lives is that our dependence on constant stimulation makes it difficult to maintain goals after they have lost their newness. After a while, when the inspiration starts to decline and our mood is flat, there is an inclination to turn to something else as a goal, something that can provide us with a new injection of inspiration. This is the same pattern of behavior we uncovered in *The Greener Grass Syndrome* of Chapter Five. This behavior is detrimental to stability. You might find yourself swinging from one goal to another until you've reached the end of your rope.

I know that when the latest goal is knocking at your door courting you with new promises, it can be exceedingly difficult to stick to an existing goal that seems to be yesterday's news. When we discussed willpower back in Chapter four, we talked about its most important ingredient—the idea that your ultimate goal behind all of this effort to maintain willpower is your metaphysical health, not the goal itself. When your focus is diverted away from the immediate goal and is aimed first and foremost at the broader principle of metaphysical health, you will no longer feel like you have to pigeon-hole your convictions in myriad different directions. Having one sturdy, unchanging focus that really encompasses everything, it is possible that you could live your whole life without ever feeling the need to fundamentally change that. In turn, the individual goals subordinate to that focus tend to remain in place. The greater the sense of stability, the greater the sense of calm. You're not going to jump at every twist and turn just because there are news flashes blazing across your radar screen every so often demanding that you reformat your entire operations.

Physical health goals, for example, wax and wane with the latest research stats and emerging trends. Usually when the latest revolution waxes with brilliant luster, the previous one wanes into dark obscurity. You might find that it's not just your waistline that becomes like a yo-yo, but—with this continuous need to redefine your goals—your mind. There is no more effective tool in the hands of the *Nefesh* than that entrapment—that back and forth rally between goals. Of course, the media, with its ever-changing logos and jingles only speeds up the confusion until it feels like you're the ping-pong ball caught between the paddles of table-tennis champions.

But if your overall goal is firmly in place, embedded in a tamper-proof box that says, "All my goals roll into this one," you will shrug your shoulders at all the outside noise blaring from the billboards and the book clubs, approaching each new fad with a sense of caution and maturity, browsing what it has to offer rather than launching yourself at it impulsively. And if, after critical evaluation, you figure you can *use it as a tool* toward your metaphysical health, then you figure out a way to gingerly insert it into your daily regimen so that it doesn't knock you off balance. This is a much healthier alternative to the electrically-charged goal setting common in our culture today.

Fill-in:

This is where you fill in your personal areas of challenge relating to goal setting on The Satellite Map. They are the "Inclusions" we spoke of in the last chapter.

The following are examples or ideas for Inclusions that you could use or build on if you relate to them:

- I make spontaneous New Year resolutions without seriously evaluating their pros and cons.
- My goals are usually designed around the latest trends in media.
- I tend to automatically expect everyone else to adapt to my goals.
- I have trouble sustaining goals that I set.
- I have trouble determining what my goals are in the first place.

For our sample chart below, I selected two Inclusions from the above list: *I tend to automatically expect everyone else to adapt to my goals*, and *I have trouble sustaining goals that I set*, and filled in the chart based on these two challenges.

Try to fit whatever your Inclusions are into the following sub-categories, really a digest of what we uncovered in this chapter:

- **Heart-led Goals:** the impulse to set goals without evaluating their overall impact.
- **Difficulty in Setting Goals:** The inability to prioritize because of the density of the information.
- **Follow-through problems:** Difficulty in sustaining current goals against the current of newer goals and ideas.

Those sub-categories that are highlighted in bold (which you can circle in red ink) are the Nerve Centers, your most profound areas of challenge. The two Inclusions in this sample belong to those Nerve Centers.

Umbrella 6: Goal Control

SUBCATEGORIES		**Heart-led Goals** Difficulty in Setting Goals **Follow-through Problems**
INCLUSIONS	SUCCESS?	I tend to automatically expect everyone else to adapt to my goals. I have trouble sustaining goals that I set.
DAY 1 OBSERVATIONS	✔ ✘	I heard about a highly innovative way to make money last week. Today I consulted with my wife first BEFORE developing my resolve to follow this plan. But I found myself trying to "push the sale" – I realized I had really made up my mind already. This is tricky.
DAY 2 OBSERVATIONS	✘	My wife reminded me of a previous scheme I had been throughly passionate about and subsequently lost interest in. I tried to stir up the excitement again, but wasn't able to.
DAY 3 OBSERVATIONS	✔ ✔	I drew up a list of pros and cons for my new goal and showed it to my family.
DAY 4 OBSERVATIONS	✘ ✘	I seemed to find a way to disprove all the suggestions made by family to amend the list. An argument then arose.
DAY 5 OBSERVATIONS	✘	I felt like giving up on the goal altogether since I was getting resistance.
DAY 6 OBSERVATIONS	✔ ✔ ✔	OK, so today I realized I was being a martyr for completely giving up just because they offered their suggestions. I actually apologized and agreed to consider their suggestions.
DAY 7 OBSERVATIONS	✘	I thought of a new idea that would trump the first. My follow-through definitely needs work.

13

Step 10: The Happy Factor

The Sitcom Syndrome

I'M GOING TO MAKE A BOLD STATEMENT (surprise, surprise):

There are many people who will go through their entire lives without recognizing happiness.

"Now hang on," you say, before I go on my maddeningly merry way. "If ever there was a perfect example of subjectivity, happiness would surely fit the mold. There are as many definitions of happiness as there are people. What makes one person happy might make another sad.... Happiness is in the eye of the...."

Yes, yes, yes. Your list is endless. If happiness is so subjective, how could I claim that there are many people who could go their whole lives without recognizing it? It's as if I am dismissing their definitions of happiness. You're right. I am. And while you're throwing tomatoes at me, I'll take the opportunity to tell you why.

When you pick up a pamphlet for a beach vacation, what do you notice about the facial expressions of the family bouncing about in the turquoise water bathing the golden sand? Elated. Thrilled. Ecstatic. Now think back to your latest actual experience of a beach vacation. What do you remember about the facial expressions of your family bouncing about in the (crowded) waters bathing the (scalding hot) sand? Pleased. Ho-hum. Frowning against the glare. Does the vacation ever match up to the pamphlet? Very rarely.

It's possible that the *idea* of the vacation is far more thrilling than the actual experience of it. Why is this so? Why do we put down a whole bundle of cash and count down a whole month of days towards an experience that turns out to be mediocre as, say, compared to utopia. And we do it again and again. Wash, rinse, repeat, never seeming to learn from our experiences.

That's because there doesn't seem to be any (non-narcotic or alcoholic) alternative. It is all but etched into the western psyche that happiness is generated through some form of external stimulation: beach vacation, fine restaurant, overseas tour, beautiful view, music concert, computer program, book, movie, art, Super-bowl, fair, relationship.... The last one here is tricky, because although relationships can be extremely meaningful there are many people who believe that just *the right relationship* will "make them happy."

This is the error underscoring so much of the current thinking: that all of these pursuits will make us happy. Although we might laugh heartily and dance and jump up and down at various intervals during these experiences, it's reactionary behavior. It's nothing more than a stimulus-response type of happiness that will fade as soon as the source fades. If the happiness lasts only as long as the instrument that tickles you, that cannot be real happiness. Genuine happiness must remain even when the source of the "happiness" disappears.

The concept of temporal happiness is the backbone behind most forms of entertainment, especially what we could call "The Sitcom Syndrome." A perfectly synchronized script together with a cast of fabulously funny characters provides for screechingly funny entertainment for half an hour (including commercials). It's a wonderful escape, and even billed as such. Let's just think about that for a bit: When you escape from a particular place, what does that say about how happy you are in that place? How is it possible that experiencing an escape can help you retain happiness in the place you escaped from? There's an almost tangible admission of this idea reflected in our own behavior: Have you ever let out a long-drawn out sigh when the credits to the sit-com come up? Sometimes when the sitcom ends, that disappointment is like your favorite ice-cream gone sour.

The laughter can certainly be very deceptive. I know a speaker who can have the audience rolling on the floor virtually as soon as he gets up to speak. He is not just funny. He is side-splitting, the kind of funny that should come with a warning to asthma sufferers. And yet, from repeated observations of his behavior outside of (and even during) "funny time," he seems to me to be not just unhappy, but well, dare I say, depressed? Is this a contradiction? Perhaps under a conventional definition of happiness this would be a glaring contradiction. How could someone so upbeat, so capable of looking at the funny side of life, so capable of laughing and inducing laughter about all of life's quirks possibly be depressed? However, if we were to redefine happiness as an internally generated feeling, there would be no contradiction. The fact that this person knows how to laugh and make others laugh has nothing to do with what's going on inside him. If a person is not succeeding with all the steps we have outlined in The Soul Diet, there can be deep internal dissatisfaction, aching confusion, and utter chaos tearing at him even as the comic delivers his punchline.

What is the exact nature of this internal happiness? It is not necessarily a mind-state induced by meditation or rhythmic breathing. It is simply the acceptance of a very central principle we mentioned in Chapter two:

There is no happiness like the resolution of doubt.

The resolution to bring our lives into a healthy focus creates a sense of internal calm. This feeling of knowing what we need to do with our lives, especially how to deal with our challenges with honesty and integrity, is real happiness. Happiness is not an escape from our challenges.

Neither is it necessarily the resolution of those challenges. Happiness is simply the unswerving conviction to deal with our challenges. Navigating the battle between the *Nefesh* and the *Neshamah* is the core of life, and when you apply this principle uniformly to all areas of your life, you are metaphysically healthy. You are happy. Always. Instead of waiting for happiness to happen to you, you are living it at every moment. You are no longer trying to be happy in spite of your challenges, you are being happy by means of your challenges.

Am I implying that you should stop going on vacation, listening to music, traveling the world? No. I'm only asking you to think of those things as a little dessert, not the source of your happiness. They cannot be the source. The vacation will never be the same as the pamphlet. The beautiful view is… you know, nice. Restaurant dining is… satiating. They are not the answer you will always be waiting for. They are the dessert when you are sure about what you're having for your main meal.

As you made your way through this book, it may have been difficult to imagine me talking about happiness, especially as I put you through grueling inner surgery. But, I hope, now you will begin to appreciate what we said in the beginning: that if anyone offers you true spirituality or happiness on a silver platter without the hard work, one that you can download onto your internal hard drive with a simple click of the button, you should be suspicious. It's the spiritual equivalent of spam. Real lasting happiness is that feeling of contentment that you worked hard for, and that you continue to work hard for. The challenges are great, but then the level of happiness is very intense. It can become so deeply rooted that nothing can ever take it away from you, no matter what happens. It is impossible to describe the beauty of this feeling. If you have reached this point in the book, you will understand what I mean.

The Freedom Trap

While we are so busy redefining things, we may as well put the concept of freedom through the ringer. The freedom plaque is also painted with rosy hues, an imagined state of bliss without strictures, a dimensionless dimension where one can run wild amongst the daisies. The irony is that this definition of freedom can actually lead to a peculiar feeling—that you are, well—*trapped?* Yes, I know, I'm at it again. Now how am I going to explain this one—that freedom is actually entrapment?

In his book, *The Paradox of Choice,*[1] Professor Barry Schwartz of Swathmore College argues that the multitude of choices and varieties facing the consumer in today's world actually increases our stress and anxiety, rather than making it easier on us. Instead of a narrow field of products and paths to choose from, the consumer now feels the pressure of making the right choice from amongst a plethora of possible right choices. So much time and energy now goes into decision-making that it can be mentally draining, and the resulting anxiety can lead to depression.

---

[1] (New York: Harper Perennial, 2005).

As you have observed, The Soul Diet takes that a step further. It's not only the increase in choices offered us that causes us confusion, but the inundation of all imagery, all slogans, all platitudes and all heart-generated impulses reducing our minds to mush. We are mush-minded people strolling the isles of choice, saying "Ooh, look at this. But, aah, look at that"—until our time on this planet has expired. Watching us through a one-way mirror, our *Nefesh* is having a field day. With one touch-sensitive stroke of a key, our *Nefesh* turns us this way and that like a puppet with short-term memory loss.

True freedom, is not, therefore throwing yourself in a thousand different directions depending on what strikes your fancy at that particular moment. When the *Nefesh* is controlling you effortlessly, that cannot possibly be freedom. You are, in fact, a slave to your whims. How free does the cheater on a diet feel with that illicit bite into a chocolate cake? How free does the gossiper feel when tearing apart her best friend behind her back? How free does the happily-married man feel when giving in to his secretary's advances? All of this is a dark pleasure that indulges the *Nefesh*, leaving behind an acrid taste of remorse in its wake. Clearly, rather than a liberated sense of expression, this is a very distressing feeling of entrapment.

Give the *Neshamah* a fighting chance here and you will gain a sense of true freedom. When the dieter is able to refuse that chocolate cake, when the gossiper is able to stem the flow of words, when the happily married man is able to resist his secretary's advances, the *Nefesh* may cry foul for a moment or two but then that feeling starts to settle in, that unmistakably beautiful feeling that you're...*free!* Free at last—because you are in control. You are not a slave to your whims. Your *Neshamah* is glowing with its latest victory. Because deep down you would never mean to sabotage your healthy diet; you would never mean to turn your back on your best friend; you would never mean to jeopardize a marriage to someone who means more to you than anyone in the world. Deep down, you are desperate to maintain these things. If it happens that you do veer from this path, that you do succumb to your whims, you might be as confused and shocked at your actions as anyone else. You're asking the same question as the others around you: *Now why would you go ahead and do that?*

It's not because you want to. You're "trapped" by yourself. And what's more, you're told by the media moguls to celebrate your freedom by embracing your whims, by following your heart. In reality, instead of celebrating your freedom you're signing away your willpower, your noble goals, your convictions.

Thus the two kinds of happiness we talked about above, temporal happiness and self-generated genuine happiness resurface when discussing the concept of freedom. The superficial thrill, the momentary exploration of one's desires against your better judgment, cannot possibly provide you with a deep sense of contentment, despite the almost tangible pleasure you might experience when engaged in these actions. True freedom, and its accompanying sense of happiness, results from your conscientious efforts to keep yourself focused, to keep yourself traveling safely along your metaphysical health track.

A New Angle on Depression

Pharmaceutical companies have built enterprises on this modern-day malady. Depression is experienced by almost eight million people in any one month period.[2] By the year 2020, it is predicted to be the second greatest cause of premature death and disability worldwide.[3] The exponential increase in depression in recent decades may very well be linked to the problems this book was created to address. Spiritual clutter, addiction to media, tightly-packed schedules going nowhere, fixation on temporal "issues of the day," "altruistic" illusions of grandeur, desensitization to intimacy, impulsive goal setting and distorted perceptions of freedom are only some of the contributing factors to our almost complete sense of disorientation. This disorientation causes depression.

As we have done with other concepts we have discussed, it will benefit us to explore this point further not from a diagnostic point of view, but from a general theoretical perspective on the very roots of depression.

In *Living Inspired*,[4] Rabbi Akiva Tatz provides illuminating insights into the concept of depression. In essence, depression results from inactive and non-creative living, a nagging sense that we are not truly engaging in life. When a human being feels that he is not engaging in life, he has arrived at the foothills of life's opposite. Death is the ultimate inactivity. In fact, the Hebrew term for a person who has died is *niftar*, literally, exempt—no longer infused with a mission to accomplish. A meticulous definition of *inactivity* is warranted here. You could be moving, but that would still be considered inactive. Do you remember the treadmill concept? When you are alive, but not living the way you were designed to, you might sense a peculiar emptiness, somewhat ominous, as if you were approaching the outer limits of death. Not quite dead. Not quite alive. It is not co-incidental that suicide has unfortunately been the "next step" for people suffering from major clinical depression. When circling so close to death, it's doesn't seem like such an extreme measure anymore.

It is also no accident that mid-life crisis is often a harbinger of depression, considering the fact that one's entire life direction comes into question: *Where am I going here with this? I am not where I imagined myself to be.* Whenever it feels as if the wheels are spinning and no progress is made, depression shows up as the uninvited guest.[5]

I'm not going to be so brazen as to claim that following the steps of this book will save your life. But I will say that I am passing on information to you that can profoundly impact your approach to your life. The severe disorientation resulting from the morass of images and philosophies we've touched on makes it very difficult to live life without direction and focus. And living life without

---

[2] The California Psychological Association, 2000.

[3] The World Health Organization, 1998.

[4] (Jerusalem: Targum Press, 1993), 153.

[5] I discuss this subject in greater depth in my forthcoming book, *Spiritual Pension Planning; Planning for Maturity with Maturity.*

direction and focus is essentially not living life. Human beings crave focus. We crave direction. These are as vital to life as the air we breathe. If a healthy focus and direction are absent, depression swoops in, the antechamber of death. As Professor Ernest Keen[6] describes it, "Depression seems to lie as an inherent counter pole to struggle and growth, much like death is the counter pole of life."

Don't let anybody tell you that happiness comes from a dilution of focus, where you broaden your mind as wide as a football field to embrace myriad alternatives. No. Nada. Your *Neshamah* groans at the thought. You will get depressed. Rather, if you resolve to clear the spiritual clutter, identify your challenges and recognize them as opportunities for growth, you will be embracing life and all it has to offer, moving steadily forward on a growth curve throughout your entire life. That is what your *Neshamah* craves. That is what you crave deep down. That is what makes you tick.

Activate!

Once you understand that true happiness is a function of dealing with and not escaping your challenges, you can consciously decide to be happy. Who ever imagined that happiness required no outside conditions to be met before you'd be able to feel it? Who ever imagined that happiness does not have to be put on hold until a certain something has to happen? Who ever thought that happiness would be at your command right now? This should bear no resemblance to the Bobby McFerron credo of "Don't worry, be happy," with its escapist connotations—Don't worry about your challenges, be happy anyway.

I respectfully disagree with that proposition. I propose that of course you should worry about your challenges. If you decide to hum a tune and play Solitaire instead of opening your credit card bill, you are not happy—you're pleasantly distracted from life. You can imagine what I have to say about a prolonged state of pleasant distraction from life. The people at AA and other rehabilitation groups will have reams of paper to read to you about the dangers of choosing such a state.

You should worry about your challenges to the extent that you need to learn how to deal with them and to confront them. Once you recognize that they are there for your growth, you have activated your potential for real happiness. I see some of you raising your hand in objection. Am I saying that we should be happy all of the time, even when we are suffering loss, God forbid, or experiencing a very difficult illness?

We all know how tough it is to deal with this issue. This subject tugs at the consciousness of so many millions of people who cannot fathom (and rightly so) why—because it absolutely defies human logic—certain things happen to them. Because of its scope, this subject really deserves separate treatment, and I hesitate to go into much depth in this forum. However, I will say that there are courageous individuals who have sculpted their outlook according to the ideals we have

---

[6] Professor Emeritus of Psychology at Bucknell University, in *Depression, Self-Consciousness, Pretending and Guilt*, (Westport, Connecticut: Praeger, 2002), 49.

set forth in this book, and who have gone beyond simply "coming to terms" with their suffering, to a point at which they see their challenges as having been deliberately placed in their path for their own self-growth. In other words, they make no attempt to understand the logic behind these challenges, but accept them as necessary phases of self-development. Are they happy even at these moments? The answer is, yes. Remember that our chosen definition of happiness is closer to contentment and inner peace than merriment and laughter.

It is possible to be in mourning but still be cognizant on some very deep level that even this challenge is placed in our path for our ultimate benefit. In fact, Torah law encourages expression of grief through very specific requirements of mourning. It may seem paradoxical that one can be "happy" even as one weeps bitterly about a very traumatic loss. But if we keep strictly to our new definition of happiness as an underlying sense of purpose and willingness to grow, the two concepts can operate concurrently. Sad and full of grief, yes. But lost? No.

As I mentioned, these are courageous individuals, some of whom I have had the privilege of meeting. I realize that it is unrealistic for me to expect you to imitate that behavior in ten easy steps. I'm not asking you to become a spiritual superhero. I'm merely pointing out that it is theoretically possible to develop that innate sense of happiness at all times, even when it seems inappropriate. At the very least you might accept the possibility of a genuine concept of happiness—a state that has no requirement of laughter, no need for jovial ho-ho-ho's but rather a profound sense of peace that this all is running according to plan.

Some people are as bubbly as a soda fountain on the exterior, but are in disarray on the interior. Others will offer only subtle displays of joy on the exterior but be filled with contentment and purpose on the inside. It is the latter group that we would want to model.

This week you will try to put this perspective into immediate action as best you can. In other words, I am asking you to try (and I only mean try) to consciously decide to be happy now. You have been brave enough to reach this point in the book. You've undertaken a media fast and a schedule slimming to give your mind a respite from the spiritual clutter. That enabled you to zoom in on your weaknesses and challenges. You've performed a very crucial inner surgery where you've confronted your raw self. You then had the all-clear to make commitments in all areas affecting your metaphysical health.

You made a commitment to the right kind of order and fitness, a commitment to anger control, a commitment to speech control, a commitment to the right kind of giving, a commitment to the right kind of intimacy, a commitment to setting the right kind of goals, and my final request is that you make this commitment—one that is the culmination of all your hard work thus far—to be happy. The real happiness, not the candy-coated one. The happiness that will remain with you for the rest of your life if you keep working at it. If you do, I will relinquish my role as your drill sergeant, because you will have joined the ranks of the truly happy. You won't need my instruction anymore.

Fill-ins

This is where you fill in your personal areas of challenge relating to happiness on The Satellite Map. They are the "Inclusions" we spoke of in the last chapter.

The following are examples or ideas for Inclusions that you could use or build on if you relate to them:

- I'm always buying things to make myself happy
- I've convinced myself that if only I could find the right partner/job/apartment, I'd be happy
- I live for weekends. That's my time for happiness
- Tragedy has stolen my ability to be happy
- I wallow in my depression without feeling the will to get out of it.

For our sample chart below, I selected two Inclusions from the above list: *I've convinced myself that if only I could find the right partner/ job/ apartment, I'd be happy*, and *Tragedy has stolen my ability to be happy*, and filled in the chart based on these two challenges.

Try to fit whatever your Inclusions are into the following sub-categories, which are really a digest of what we uncovered in this chapter:

- **Waiting to be Happy:** A perception of happiness as a product of external stimulation, and thus waiting for happiness to descend.
- **The Freedom Trap:** A distorted perception of freedom as a paradigm of boundless choice only contributes to confusion.
- **Depression:** Lacking firm direction leads to disorientation, in turn leading to this state.

Those sub-categories that are highlighted in bold (which you can circle in red ink) are the Nerve Centers, your most profound areas of challenge. The two Inclusions in this sample belong to those Nerve Centers.

Umbrella 7: The Happy Factor

SUBCATEGORIES	**Waiting to be Happy** The Freedom Trap Depression **Continous Happiness**

INCLUSIONS	SUCCESS?	I've convinced myself that if only I could find the right partner/job/apartment, I'd be happy. Tragedy has stolen my ability to be happy.
DAY 1 OBSERVATIONS	✔ ✘	While in the department store I resisted the temptation to buy a new set of garden furniture on sale, but then splurged on a new silverware set, even though I didn't need it.
DAY 2 OBSERVATIONS	✘	I almost refuse to be happy because of that event in my family four years ago.
DAY 3 OBSERVATIONS	✔ ✔	Today I thought about all of the things I DO have, and also realized just how deceiving that feeling of lacking is.
DAY 4 OBSERVATIONS	✘ ✘	I was thinking today if I could just get a better job I would be able to feel happier. I seem to crave distraction, thinking it can help me deal with my pain.
DAY 5 OBSERVATIONS	✘	Everybody has iPods these days. I resent being left behind.
DAY 6 OBSERVATIONS	✔ ✔ ✔	For a few moments today I was able to view the struggles in my life as having improved me. I told myself to be happy because it is within my power. I tried to hold onto that feeling for as long as I could.
DAY 7 OBSERVATIONS	✘	I sat watching sitcom after sitcom this evening and couldn't get up – it's that distraction thing again.

14

After the Diet

A MOUNTAIN-CLIMBER MIGHT FACE AN UNEXPECTED DILEMMA as he reaches the peak. For hours and hours he has struggled, stretching every sinew as he inched his way up the craggy rock-face. A vision of the illustrious summit carried him upwards at every step of the way. Now he's done it. He's finally at the top. The question is *what now?*

When you are steadfastly making your way toward a clearly defined goal, the attainment of that goal often brings with it a sudden feeling of disorientation. There's a sense that something is lacking now that you're off that very clearly defined track. This is a possible outcome of reaching the end of this diet. It's been several weeks now that you have plugged yourself into a neatly packaged spiritual rehabilitation program that has enabled you to quantify who you are in almost empirical form. You've reduced your insides to a drawing board of plusses and minuses, sorted your idiosyncrasies into various inboxes and outboxes and souped up many of your neglected functions. Are you expected to just blend into your previous way of life armed with all this knowledge? Isn't it like trying to bring a math text book to a poetry class? Life is not a rigid ten step program. It flows like freestyle verse. How will you be able to carry a structured, methodical course of self-study such as *The Soul Diet* into the rest of your life? Are you expected to keep ledgers forever?

This is our cue to open up The Satellite Map in its entirety. Now that it is all filled in, you have a giant record of your most pertinent struggles as well as of your most noteworthy successes during each week of focus. There is something very satisfying about seeing yourself physically mapped out like that, all in one capsule for you to peruse as though you were checking out the topography of your mind. Rather than having to sift through a tangle of isolated ideas and tidbits you've garnered over the years from disparate ends of the earth, there you have it laid out methodically in front of you in a carefully engineered report.

Now, instead of looking at each umbrella as an isolated entity, you are able to view all the umbrellas together and start to compare notes on each one. Do you find that there may be a common thread or two underlying certain patterns of behavior across the spectrum? Do you notice, for example, that it was as difficult for you to succeed in maintaining an ordered house or office as it was to regulate what type of speech to use and when? Is it possible that the two seemingly unrelated areas actually stem from a common problem? An inability to sort through your physical stuff just might be related to an inability to sort through your verbal stuff.

Do you notice that your unwillingness to reduce your obsession with your career is just as intense as your unwillingness to reduce your obsession with a particular exercise regimen? An inability to think outside of yourself in terms of your career just might be related to an inability to think outside of yourself in terms of your physical health.

In comparing and contrasting the different umbrellas, you will thus gain a richer perspective of yourself than you did by analyzing each area separately. Guard this Satellite Map well. Although you are now "finished" with your diet, you will always be able to refer to the map to remind yourself what needs to be worked on, what needs redefining, what is truly important to you. Even without this weekly focus, you're still able to put yourself back in the chart for a moment or two to regain that clarity of focus you had while you were developing the chart. Once you've done the Soul Diet, it will be possible to simply "bring up" the area of focus because you have it stored somewhere in your memory banks. For example:

– You're in the middle of a chat over coffee with your friend, and you're about to launch into a really unnecessary diatribe about a work associate who serves no other purpose than to provide some action-packed verbal entertainment for the two of you to savor. You suddenly recall the week you spent working on Speech Control. You mentally zone in on the designated area of your Satellite Map as if you are tracing the "You Are Here" X on a mall layout map. Placing yourself back in that context, you make a valiant attempt to restrain yourself from the imminent outpour. Even if you don't succeed, you have at least made the attempt, and you will try to do better next time.

– You are diligently at work on your computer in the library when someone right next to you diligently working on their computer begins to hum a Bee Gees tune in suitably high pitch, not loud enough to be classified as officially disturbing the silence, but loud enough to cause the nerves along your spine to break-dance. As the indignation and anger begins to build, you start to recognize your reaction as a symptom of self-worship, a distinct category within the umbrella of Anger Control on The Satellite Map that relates this type of anger to idol-worship, since both share a clear, undiluted manifesto: *I want things to go my way, and no-one dare spoil my equilibrium.* At that point you perk up and the anger starts to subside—you're saying to yourself: Well, why do I expect this person to automatically conform to my thinking?

On the other hand, if you do put aside The Satellite Map, letting it lie somewhere unused, probably there will be a disconnect—you will be less likely to link your current specific behavior and attitude to what you learned while on the diet, or to regress to an earlier state of confusion. So, even if you are no longer following a weekly schedule, it is important to always consult your Satellite Map.

Some of you, however, will opt to continue with the format of the diet by repeating the whole sequence so that it becomes an eighteen-week-program, a twenty-seven week program, a thirty-six week program, and so on. This, of course, means enduring another two-week Media Fast and Schedule Slimming as well as filling out a new Satellite Map each time.[1] If you are disciplined enough to do this, I highly recommend it for a variety of reasons:

1. Repeating the steps you took to correct your behavior will serve to reinforce your changed ways.

2. There were so many instances where you felt if you only had more time to work on a specific issue than just one week you'd have made substantial progress, but you were forced to start the next week's focus. Now you have the opportunity to build on what you began.

3. There are certain elements that are virtually impossible to correct in just one week. To name a few:

    – Completely organizing your office, house, and time schedule
    – Trimming your weight and becoming physically fit
    – Reducing your speech to only constructive, honest expression
    – Reshaping your entire approach to intimacy and modesty
    – Altering your approach to your suffering.

4. You may feel that in each week your regression claimed back any progress you made. Every time you tried to succeed you made only marginal gains on the one hand and succumbed so quickly on the other. No doubt about it—this is a difficult diet. When we spoke about regression in Chapter Six, we stated that swings are perfectly natural. Not only that, but the regression itself is a challenge of its own. It is there simply to discourage you. It is not so much that you may have failed your challenge that is critical, but whether or not you fight that feeling of despondency. By repeating the course of The Soul Diet, you will be able to transfer that conviction into action. Even though you regressed previously, you will want to work on it until you make good progress.

Whether you decide to go for a second or third round of The Soul Diet, or whether you feel you are sufficiently equipped with what you need to continue your path toward metaphysical health on your own, either of these options is certainly better than not doing The Soul Diet at all.

Obviously, it is not possible to tailor a book to each and every individual's idiosyncrasies, motivations, goals and personal history. I have tried to make the book as universally accessible as possible, taking into account differing permutations of character and personal challenge. But there will often remain unanswered questions in your mind, questions that begin with, "Yeah, but what if…." And naturally I am not there to answer you.

---

[1] See Models of Integration in Appendix 1 for more details.

■

Postscript

It is not possible to tailor a book to each and every individual's idiosyncrasies, motivations, goals and personal history. Taking into account differing permutations of character and personal challenge, I have tried to make the book as universally accessible as possible. Of course there will often remain unanswered questions in your mind, questions that begin with, "Yeah, but what if…" And naturally I am not there to answer you.

I plan to conduct workshops on The Soul Diet where you will have the opportunity to approach me personally. I will try to give you as much individual attention there as I can. As well, I plan to offer private consultations and Soul Diet counseling.

My web site will naturally be a mixed blessing. If you are capable of limiting your time on the Internet to gaining what you can from the site, then you will benefit from the information there. But if you are not quite as disciplined as that, I ask you *not* to visit my website. (Bet that's a new one for you.) I don't want to endanger your metaphysical health in the process of improving your metaphysical health! Some of you may have initially learned about this book through my website, but now that you've been on the diet you might think of yourself as having crossed over to the other side—you know better now. You're too responsible and directed to risk losing your focus. Instead, if you'd like to receive updates about upcoming workshops in your area, how to obtain free Satellite Maps or other info, please call or write using the information on the *contact* page.

As I am no longer your drill sergeant, I have a few concluding words to say about you, the reader. As I mentioned at the beginning, much of the content of this book stems from sources abounding in age-old wisdom—I just happened to have collated them in an accessible format. Having incorporated some of this sage advice into your daily life, you have allowed yourself to tap into wisdom that transcends centuries—to broaden your perspective beyond your immediate knowledge base and to begin to rethink some previously unquestioned modern-day dictums. What may have been set in stone in your mind since the day you were born, not to overlook some questionable conventional mentality picked up along the way, might very well have given way to the timeless knowledge infused into the world since the day it was created. You've gone beyond yourself by being prepared to face yourself. You've accepted the challenge to deal with your challenges and not avoid them. You've had the courage to begin what may seem a formidable task, but one, it is hoped, that you will come to realize is a profoundly powerful path toward living life to its fullest.

I congratulate you for reaching this point, for not giving up and not giving in, and I hope that you are able to maintain the convictions you have developed along the way for the rest of your life.

■

Appendix I

After the Media Fast and Schedule Slimming

You've completed the two week media fast and your two week schedule slimming, and have begun working on the first couple of umbrellas. Your question is, how do you approach media and your schedule now that you've been away from it for two weeks?

Once you have experienced the sweetness of the reprieve and the clarity it affords you, you might actually not feel the need to immediately return to the full-on invasion to which you subjected yourself before you started the diet. You might not want to risk losing that tranquility.

On the other hand, full abstention will probably be quite difficult to maintain for an extended period of time. This is why the fast and the schedule slimming are essentially induction periods, helping you develop a taste for peace and quiet and enabling you to embark on your personal scrutiny. After that, you might look at how to integrate media and activities into your life so that they do not overwhelm you, so that you maintain control of them, rather than be controlled by them.

How could this work practically? Well, you would perform a process of selection based on the utility of the particular medium or activity in question. That is, you would ask yourself what benefit that particular item has for your growth and health.

For example:

1. There is a web site with helpful information on how to organize your desk, your timetable, or your shopping lists more efficiently.
2. There is a film or television program with a very poignant message that provides insight into life's challenges
3. There is a local news channel that provides traffic, weather and market information that will actually save you a good deal of time and expense if you listen to it.
4. You find that the sitcom on television has the effect of relaxing you so that you function better. NOTE: You are not looking to the sitcom as a source of happiness.
   (See Chapter 13.)

5. You have spare time to help with the PTA at your kid's school, and it does not interfere with your family time.
6. You're not succumbing to the "Greener Grass Syndrome." You really believe that switching your job will allow you to have stronger metaphysical health.
7. By being a member of your local book club, you find that it relaxes you every time you meet so that you are able to function better, and your family fully supports your doing this.

Whatever the case may be, it is up to you to remember not to lose yourself in that particular medium or activity so that you find yourself gravitating to your old habits. If you find it difficult to break away from the computer once you've sat down to innocently check your email, you might want to keep that restriction you imposed on yourself doing the Media Fast to check your email standing or to remove the chair altogether while you do it.

Again, it's your discretion needed here. You need to be aware of your limitations so that you will know what you are capable of handling. But hopefully that two week respite from the media and heavy schedule will have made you stronger and more open to the idea of stemming the stimulus invasion.

Models of Integration:

The Soul Diet is really a flexible plan. (Don't fall off your seat. Just give me a chance.) Although each step itself is non-negotiable, there can be variations in how you implement the program, depending on your preferences. We already mentioned at the end of The Schedule Slimming in Chapter 5 that there are some options in deciding how to manage the Schedule Slimming with the Media Fast. We mentioned that deciding when to start the Schedule Slimming will depend on how well you are surviving the Media Fast. If you find you begin the Media Fast and your withdrawal symptoms are mild—you're dealing with it well—then take on the two week period of Schedule Slimming right away. So, for example, if you begin your Media Fast on Monday the 1st and by Thursday you're doing fine, then begin the Schedule Slimming period that day and end it a few days after your Media Fast. All the rest of the steps of the diet will follow after that. So your complete Soul Diet calendar will look something like this:

☐ = The Media Fast   ▨ = Schedule Slimming

January

1	2	3	4	5	6	7	8	9	10	11	12	13	14	15

16	17	18	19	20	21	22	23	24	25	26	27	28	29	30	31

Umbrella 1: Order & Fitness   **Umbrella 2: Anger Control**

February

1	2	3	4	5	6	7	8	9	10	11	12	13	14	15

Umbrella 3: Speech Control   **Umbrella 4: The Giving Factor**

16	17	18	19	20	21	22	23	24	25	26	27	28

Umbrella 5: Intimacy   **Umbrella 6: Goal Control**

March

1	2	3	4	5	6	7	8	9	10	11	12	13	14	15

Umbrella 7: The Happy Factor

16	17	18	19	20	21	22	23	24	25	26	27	28	29	30	31

In the above scenario, you began your Media Fast on January 1st, and then took on the Schedule Slimming on January 4th. Your Media Fast ended on January 14th, but your Schedule Slimming extended to January 18th. About January 12th, toward the end of your Media Fast, you had begun to write the paragraph about yourself that we mentioned in Chapter Six. Then, on January 19th, you were done with both the Media Fast and the Schedule Slimming and ready to begin the seven umbrellas. You were done with the entire Soul Diet on March 9th.

If, on the other hand, you find you are struggling with the Media Fast, don't begin the Schedule Slimming until you are ready. However, at the very latest you should begin it the day right after you have completed your Media Fast. There should be no break between the two periods because then you run the risk of losing the momentum. Thus at this maximum allowance your complete Soul Diet Calendar would look like this:

January

1	2	3	4	5	6	7	8	9	10	11	12	13	14	15
16	17	18	19	20	21	22	23	24	25	26	27	28	29	30	31

Umbrella 1

February

1	2	3	4	5	6	7	8	9	10	11	12	13	14	15
Umbrella 1: Order & Fitness						Umbrella 2: Anger Control						Umbrella 3		
16	17	18	19	20	21	22	23	24	25	26	27	28		
Umbrella 3: Speech Control					Umbrella 4: The Giving Factor						Umbrella 5			

March

1	2	3	4	5	6	7	8	9	10	11	12	13	14	15
Umbrella 5: Intimacy						Umbrella 6: Goal Control						Umbrella 7		
16	17	18	19	20	21	22	23	24	25	26	27	28	29	30	31
Umbrella 7: Happy Factor															

In this instance, you began your Media Fast on January1st, and then took on the Schedule Slimming only at the end of your Media Fast on January 15th. Your Schedule Slimming finished on January 29th. Around January 12th, towards the end of your Media Fast, you had begun to write the paragraph about yourself. Then, on January 30th, you were done with both the Media Fast and the Schedule Slimming and ready to begin the seven umbrellas. You were done with the entire Soul Diet on March 19th.

Remember that in both cases, even after the Media Fast and Schedule Slimming, you will be working out how to slowly reconstruct your schedule and reintroduce appropriate media for what might be weeks to come, as we outlined above. So, even as you begin the umbrellas, you will still be dealing with these factors concurrently.

In addition, if you do decide to go another round of The Soul Diet as we mentioned in the final chapter, you could change the timing of the Schedule Slimming and Media Fast this time around according to your preferences.

You may also find when you look at your Satellite Map that certain umbrellas provided more of a challenge than others, and that the second time around you want to extend an umbrella by a week or more. It's advisable, though, to put some sort of limit on it or else the other umbrellas might fall by the wayside. It's better to service everything so that you will maintain balance.

■

Appendix II

On the following page you will find a completed Satellite Map comprised of all the sample charts we filled in throughout the stages of the diet. This is just to give you an idea of what your own Satellite Map might look like, and to allow you to gain some idea of the benefits of seeing a structured bird's eye-view of your mind.

The pages that follow contain blank charts for you to fill in. When you're done, cut them out and paste them together as I have done so that you will have created your own Satellite Map.

How to navigate the map:

1. Remember to keep handy that paragraph you wrote about yourself in Step 3 so that you can compare the free-flowing content of the note to the more structured content of the charts. You might notice that your paragraph encompasses some of the broader themes of many of the more detailed observations on the map. Make a note of these.

2. Now try to find comparisons between the observations in each chart in the map, noting any connecting themes and underlying patterns.

3. You will emerge with a fairly detailed overall picture of the thoughts and challenges unique to your personality and circumstance. Armed with this information you will be able to maintain a strong sense of clarity about your life's focus and direction.

An example:

Let's say the following is Phyllis Amplechart's paragraph:

> *"I find I am depressed a lot, or is it just sad? I don't do well in relationships. I don't always feel I can trust so I feel like I'm in limbo. I'm pretty smart and outgoing but I don't always know how what to do with that—I make a lot of mistakes."*

When Phyllis consults her Satellite Map she realizes that her problem with relationships is associated with the Giving Factor and Intimacy charts. She realizes from the Giving Factor that she has been "waiting to receive" a sense of security in her relationships, rather than actively building it herself. Something else dawns on her that hasn't occurred to her before. Her outgoingness has affected her "attitude towards modesty" (Intimacy) which may well have caused the uncertainty in the relationship with her husband. All this has contributed to a sense of aimlessness and "depression" (the Happy Factor) which in turn has made it difficult for her to set goals (Goal Control).

Next Phyllis compares the charts of the map to discern any common themes in her observations. She notices, for example, that the following observations from two entirely different umbrellas are likely related:

- "I decided to make my husband a special meal for dinner. But then while I was making the dinner I fixated about why he hasn't done something special for me" (The Giving Factor)
- "Had nothing but criticism for my kids today" (Speech Control)

The theme she has uncovered is an inordinate focus on what others should be doing for her, rather than what she should be doing for them. Knowing that this is a significant overarching area of challenge in life enables her to develop the tools to face it with clarity and conviction.

Umbrella 2: Anger Control

SUBCATEGORIES		Anger Geography **Self-worship** Blinkered Vision **Self-righteous Protest**
INCLUSIONS	SUCCESS?	I get very annoyed when all I get is everyone's answering machines. I constantly think that I am one of the only people in this house/business who has his head screwed on right.
DAY 1 OBSERVATIONS	✔ ✘	Although my boss didn't e-mail me what I wanted when I wanted it, I was able to contain my anger when I realized it was a demand to see things my way. But then when I saw him later I could not stop the feeling of resentment.
DAY 2 OBSERVATIONS	✘	I actually yelled at a fellow committee member, using the word "incompetent."
DAY 3 OBSERVATIONS	✔ ✔	Today I was able to come out with an apology AND a compliment for the person I yelled at yesterday, even though I felt every part of me resist it.
DAY 4 OBSERVATIONS	✘ ✘	I knew my brother was at home and STILL he wasn't picking up the phone. Not only did that make me angry, but I know he had answered my sister's call earlier because she told me she had called him. Now I was furious.
DAY 5 OBSERVATIONS	✘	I just did not feel up to battling my anger with incompetence today.
DAY 6 OBSERVATIONS	✔ ✔ ✔	OK—progress! I offered to help another committee member implement her suggestion rather than react with indignation because the suggestion wasn't mine. Then, when she smirked, I didn't react! I couldn't reach my cousin at the time we agreed to talk, but, buoyed by my convictions, I calmly tried again until I could.
DAY 7 OBSERVATIONS	✘	I had a headache and was not in the mood again for dealing with incompetence.

Umbrella 3: Speech Control

SUBCATEGORIES		**Indiscriminate and Meaningless Speech** Sarcasm Gossip and Slander **Lies**
INCLUSIONS	SUCCESS?	I'm always criticizing, but never complimenting. I tell myself that the extra money I draw from the business is really owed to me because I work so hard.
DAY 1 OBSERVATIONS	✔ ✘	I only noticed today how much I just let loose my criticism without second thought. It still didn't stop me from doing it, though.
DAY 2 OBSERVATIONS	✘	It's so hard to reverse an attitude of "the company owes me." I used the company credit card today for lunch with my wife.
DAY 3 OBSERVATIONS	✔ ✔	I actually resisted calling in "sick" so that I could go to the game. AND I didn't watch it on TV on company time, either.
DAY 4 OBSERVATIONS	✘ ✘	Whipped out the company card to pay for gas for my brother's car, and then had words for my boss who questioned where I'd been.
DAY 5 OBSERVATIONS	✘	Had nothing but criticism for my kids today.
DAY 6 OBSERVATIONS	✔ ✔ ✔	A co-worker ran an errand for me. When she returned, I made a conscious effort to thank her properly. Beforehand I found this difficult to do (I kind of expected it if she were a real friend). Then when I found out she had omitted a detail, I didn't say anything. When she walked away, I didn't even mumble under my breath.
DAY 7 OBSERVATIONS	✘	Since the company had ordered more than enough binders for its employees, I just took a few home with me. Who would miss them?

Umbrella 6: Goal Control

SUBCATEGORIES		**Heart-led Goals** Difficulty in Setting Goals **Follow-through Problems**
INCLUSIONS	SUCCESS?	I tend to automatically expect everyone else to adapt to my goals. I have trouble sustaining goals that I set.
DAY 1 OBSERVATIONS	✔ ✘	I heard about a highly innovative way to make money last week. Today I consulted with my wife first BEFORE developing my resolve to follow this plan. But I found myself trying to "push the sale" – I realized I had really made up my mind already. This is tricky.
DAY 2 OBSERVATIONS	✘	My wife reminded me of a previous scheme I had been throughly passionate about and subsequently lost interest in. I tried to stir up the excitement again, but wasn't able to.
DAY 3 OBSERVATIONS	✔ ✔	I drew up a list of pros and cons for my new goal and showed it to my family.
DAY 4 OBSERVATIONS	✘ ✘	I seemed to find a way to disprove all the suggestions made by family to amend the list. An argument then arose.
DAY 5 OBSERVATIONS	✘	I felt like giving up on the goal altogether since I was getting resistance.
DAY 6 OBSERVATIONS	✔ ✔ ✔	OK, so today I realized I was being a martyr for completely giving up just because they offered their suggestions. I actually apologized and agreed to consider their suggestions.
DAY 7 OBSERVATIONS	✘	I thought of a new idea that would trump the first. My follow-through definitely needs work.

Umbrella 7: The Happy Factor

SUBCATEGORIES		**Waiting to be Happy** The Freedom Trap Depression **Continous Happiness**
INCLUSIONS	SUCCESS?	I've convinced myself that if only I could find the right partner/job/apartment, I'd be happy. Tragedy has stolen my ability to be happy.
DAY 1 OBSERVATIONS	✔ ✘	While in the department store I resisted the temptation to buy a new set of garden furniture on sale, but then splurged on a new silverware set, even though I didn't need it.
DAY 2 OBSERVATIONS	✘	I almost refuse to be happy because of that event in my family four years ago.
DAY 3 OBSERVATIONS	✔ ✔	Today I thought about all of the things I DO have, and also realized just how deceiving that feeling of lacking is.
DAY 4 OBSERVATIONS	✘ ✘	I was thinking today if I could just get a better job I would be able to feel happier. I seem to crave distraction, thinking it can help me deal with my pain.
DAY 5 OBSERVATIONS	✘	Everybody has iPods these days. I resent being left behind.
DAY 6 OBSERVATIONS	✔ ✔ ✔	For a few moments today I was able to view the struggles in my life as having improved me. I told myself to be happy because it is within my power. I tried to hold onto that feeling for as long as I could.
DAY 7 OBSERVATIONS	✘	I sat watching sitcom after sitcom this evening and couldn't get up – it's that distraction thing again.

THE SATELLITE MAP

This is an example of what a completed Satellite Map might look like. To fill in your own, fill in the charts at the end of this book, cut them out and place them together as a unit.

Alternatively order your FREE (excl. shipping) already-made large Satellite Map for easy fill-in by calling **866.SOULDIET** or by going to **SoulDiet.com**.

NOTE: A significant segment of The Soul Diet workshops is dedicated to detailed analysis of The Satellite Map. To be notified of upcoming workshops in your area please contact the publisher (see contact page).

Umbrella 1: Order & Fitness

SUBCATEGORIES	**Diet and Exercise Conviction** Maintaining Order Unhealthy Fitness, Unhealthy Order **Punctuality and Commitment Problems**	
INCLUSIONS	*SUCCESS?*	I keep switching diets thinking the new one will help me. I'm always late for work.
DAY 1 OBSERVATIONS	✔	I resisted the impulse to buy a new diet book and instead started looking up one I have already tried
DAY 2 OBSERVATIONS	✘ ✘	I only noticed today that I never show up exactly on time for anything. Even when I consider myself to be on time, it's always a couple of minutes late. I miscalculate the amount of time needed to get somewhere on time.
DAY 3 OBSERVATIONS	✔ ✔	I left very early for both of my meetings today, and was surprised to find that I arrived only 5 minutes early both times. But it felt good, I was in control.
DAY 4 OBSERVATIONS	✘	It's difficult to maintain enthusiam for a diet that nobody else is doing anymore.
DAY 5 OBSERVATIONS	✔	I was never so conscious of how inconsiderate it is to be late for appointments. Today was an eye-opener for me.
DAY 6 OBSERVATIONS	✔ ✔ ✔	I really focused today. Clean house, on time, paid bills right away instead of putting them aside.
DAY 7 OBSERVATIONS	✘	Burnt out. I need to work on consistency.

Umbrella 4: The Giving Factor

SUBCATEGORIES	**Waiting to Receive** Self-Indulgent Giving **Career Immersion** Pure Taking	
INCLUSIONS	*SUCCESS?*	I look at relationships as the way the other person makes me feel or what I can get out of that person. I am obsessed with getting the most out of my career, at the expense of getting married or spending time with my family.
DAY 1 OBSERVATIONS	✔ ✘	I decided to make my husband a special meal for dinner. But then while I was making the dinner I fixated about why he hasn't done something special for me in a long time, either.
DAY 2 OBSERVATIONS	✘	I had to cancel my daughter's birthday party because a major client needed an emergency meeting with me. I know my cancellation was wrong.
DAY 3 OBSERVATIONS	✔ ✔	I worked up the courage to cancel a different meeting to make the party. Although risking a possible backlash from the client, I realized that my daughter only has one childhood with me. I spent time with her at the party rather than making sure she had her friends and her gifts so that I could disappear to make phone calls.
DAY 4 OBSERVATIONS	✘ ✘	I played this mind game where I waited to see what my husband would get me for our anniversary before I did any reciprocal shopping. And when I saw that he didn't spend that much, neither did I.
DAY 5 OBSERVATIONS	✘	I was thinking today how my sister never calls me.
DAY 6 OBSERVATIONS	✔ ✔ ✔	I decided to call my sister, without thinking afterward that it was now her turn to call me. I then put it into my calendar to call her the following week.
DAY 7 OBSERVATIONS	✘	My husband didn't want me to apply for a particular promotion, and I had trouble fighting with my ambitious drive to get to the top.

Umbrella 5: Intimacy

SUBCATEGORIES	Mechanical Relationship Desensitization **Attitude towards Modesty** **Easily Trapped**	
INCLUSIONS	*SUCCESS?*	I like to dress provocatively. I'm married but enjoy the excitement of flirting.
DAY 1 OBSERVATIONS	✔ ✘	I tried to dress more conservatively when I went out with my husband but I still caught myself talking playfully with this other guy there.
DAY 2 OBSERVATIONS	✘	It was hot today, so I succumbed and used it as an opportunity to show off my new skimpy dress, and I enjoyed the stares I got.
DAY 3 OBSERVATIONS	✔ ✔	I chose to dress modestly and felt regal! Best of all my husband appreciated my reserving my intimacy for him only.
DAY 4 OBSERVATIONS	✘ ✘	A male co-worker wanted to take me for lunch to talk about his career. From the way he asked me, I should have known that his interest stretched beyond career counseling. And the thing is, I didn't resist it, and actually enjoyed the meeting, even though I knew that it encroached on the intimacy with my husband.
DAY 5 OBSERVATIONS	✘	Everybody else was dressed provocatively, so how could I possible stand out?
DAY 6 OBSERVATIONS	✔ ✔ ✔	Not only did I turn down an "innocent" coffee with a lonely male friend, but I invited him to dinner with me and my husband so that we could talk afterwards while my husband worked in the next room. Well, what do you know? He wasn't interested in that. I learned a lot today!
DAY 7 OBSERVATIONS	✘	The idea of buying a whole new "modest" wardrobe intimidates me.

Umbrella #:

SUBCATEGORIES		
INCLUSIONS	SUCCESS?	
DAY 1 OBSERVATIONS		
DAY 2 OBSERVATIONS		
DAY 3 OBSERVATIONS		
DAY 4 OBSERVATIONS		
DAY 5 OBSERVATIONS		
DAY 6 OBSERVATIONS		
DAY 7 OBSERVATIONS		

Umbrella #:

SUBCATEGORIES		
INCLUSIONS	**SUCCESS?**	
DAY 1 OBSERVATIONS		
DAY 2 OBSERVATIONS		
DAY 3 OBSERVATIONS		
DAY 4 OBSERVATIONS		
DAY 5 OBSERVATIONS		
DAY 6 OBSERVATIONS		
DAY 7 OBSERVATIONS		

Umbrella #:

SUBCATEGORIES		
INCLUSIONS	**SUCCESS?**	
DAY 1 OBSERVATIONS		
DAY 2 OBSERVATIONS		
DAY 3 OBSERVATIONS		
DAY 4 OBSERVATIONS		
DAY 5 OBSERVATIONS		
DAY 6 OBSERVATIONS		
DAY 7 OBSERVATIONS		

Umbrella #:

SUBCATEGORIES		
INCLUSIONS	**SUCCESS?**	
DAY 1 OBSERVATIONS		
DAY 2 OBSERVATIONS		
DAY 3 OBSERVATIONS		
DAY 4 OBSERVATIONS		
DAY 5 OBSERVATIONS		
DAY 6 OBSERVATIONS		
DAY 7 OBSERVATIONS		

Umbrella #:

SUBCATEGORIES		
INCLUSIONS	**SUCCESS?**	
DAY 1 OBSERVATIONS		
DAY 2 OBSERVATIONS		
DAY 3 OBSERVATIONS		
DAY 4 OBSERVATIONS		
DAY 5 OBSERVATIONS		
DAY 6 OBSERVATIONS		
DAY 7 OBSERVATIONS		

Umbrella #:

SUBCATEGORIES		
INCLUSIONS	SUCCESS?	
DAY 1 OBSERVATIONS		
DAY 2 OBSERVATIONS		
DAY 3 OBSERVATIONS		
DAY 4 OBSERVATIONS		
DAY 5 OBSERVATIONS		
DAY 6 OBSERVATIONS		
DAY 7 OBSERVATIONS		

Umbrella #:

SUBCATEGORIES		
INCLUSIONS	**SUCCESS?**	
DAY 1 OBSERVATIONS		
DAY 2 OBSERVATIONS		
DAY 3 OBSERVATIONS		
DAY 4 OBSERVATIONS		
DAY 5 OBSERVATIONS		
DAY 6 OBSERVATIONS		
DAY 7 OBSERVATIONS		

■

Bibliography

Judaic:

Dessler, Rabbi Eliyahu E. *Michtav M'Eliyahu*. Vol. 2. Jerusalem: Sifriati,1997.

Heller, Rabbi Yehoshua. *Chosen Yehoshua*. Essay 1, Jerusalem: 1998.

Luzzato, Rabbi Moshe Chaim. *The Way of God*. Sixth Edition. Jerusalem/New York: Feldheim Publishers, 1997.

Kelemen, Rabbi Lawrence. *To Kindle a Soul*. Michigan: Targum/Feldheim, 2002.

Pliskin, Rabbi Zelig. *Gateway to Happiness*. Jerusalem: Aish HaTorah Publications, 1983.

Silverstein, Rabbi Shraga (translator). *Cheshbon HaNefesh*. Jerusalem/New York: Feldheim Publishers, 1995.

Tatz, Rabbi Akiva. *Living Inspired*. Jerusalem: Targum Press, 1993.

General:

Ackerman, Dick. "Technology and Obscenity: Ever-changing Legal Battles." *Nexus Journal*. Volume 10, 2003: 37-47.

Ali, Lorraine and Miller, Lisa. "The Secret Lives of Wives." *Newsweek*, July 12, 2004: 47.

Barnouw, Erik. *The Sponsor: Notes on a Modern Potentate*. New York: Oxford University Press, 1978.

Cornett, Carlton. *The Soul of Psychotherapy: Recapturing the Spiritual Dimension in the Therapeutic Encounter*. New York: The Free Press, 1998.

Cortright, Brant. *Psychotherapy and Spirit*. Albany: State University of New York Press, 1997.

Dreazen, Yochi J. and Silverman, Rachel Emma. "Raised in Cyberspace: Using Computers can quickly become second nature to children; that isn't necessarily such a good thing." *The Wall Street Journal Millennium (A Special Report): Politics & Society.* Dec 31, 1999: R.47.

Herman, Hank. "Question: how often do men think about sex? Answer: he's probably thinking about it right now." *Ladies Home Journal*, March 1993, v110: 98.

Hillman, James. *Revisioning Psychology.* New York: Harper & Row, 1975.

Jones, Jeffrey P. "Vox Populi as Cable Programming Strategy." *Journal of Popular Film and Television.* Heldref Publications, Spring 2003, Vol. 31, Iss. 1: 18.

Keen, Ernest. *Self-Consciousness, Pretending and Guilt.* Westport, Connecticut: Praeger, 2002.

Pollay, Richard W. "The Distorted Mirror: Reflections on the Unintended Consequences of Advertising." *Journal of Marketing.* April 1986. Vol. 50: 21.

Postman, Neil. *Amusing Ourselves to Death, Public Discourse in the Age of Show Business.* New York: Penguin Books, 1985.

Postman, Neil. *Technopoly, The Surrender of Culture to Technology.* First Edition. New York: Vintage Books, April 1993.

Schaller, Mark. "The Psychological Consequences of Fame: Three Tests of the Self-Consciousness Hypothesis." *Journal of Personality*, June 1997 65:2: 291–309.

Schwartz, Barry. *The Paradox of Choice: Why More is Less.* New York: Harper Perennial, Jan 1, 2005.

Thoreau, Henry David. *Walden.* Boston: Houghton-Mifflin, 1957.

Toye, Sue. "People Cocooning more, socializing less at home: study. Change in the use of the dwelling space result of social and demographic changes." Office of Web and Info Services, Division of University Advancement, University of Toronto, June 23, 2004.

Varan, Duane. "The Cultural Erosion Metaphor and the Transcultural Impact of Media Systems." *Journal of Communication*, Spring 1998. Vol 48. Iss. 2: 58.

Watson, John. *The Battle of Behaviorism: An Exposition and an Exposure.* New York: W.W. Norton & Co., January 1st, 1929.

■

COMING SOON:

Spiritual Pension Planning: Planning for Maturity with Maturity

By Yitzchak Goldman, Neeman House (April, 2008)

After several years of visiting residents of senior homes to offer them spiritual guidance, the author observed that 85–90% had almost no will to live, had no sense of fulfillment at having lived so many years, and that very little could be said to comfort them.

Considering the fact that baby-boomers are entering their retirement years accompanied by an artillery of life-prolonging medical innovations, the Western world faces unprecedented numbers of just such people wishing their lives away. These are people who have by and large diligently prepared financially for their retirement, their bustling portfolios of IRA's, Real Estate and Long Term Care Insurance all neatly aligned and ready for action. Yet mentally and spiritually they are woefully unprepared for doing time in the youth-centric culture surrounding them.

Just as it is too late to prepare financially for retirement when one reaches old age, it is also too late to prepare spiritually for retirement when one reached old age. Spiritual Pension Planning is the antidote to these concerns, providing practical decade-by-decade advice on how to prepare spiritually.

To be kept informed on the progress of this book and its workshop dates, please contact
info@neemanhouse.com

■

Contact

Using the information below, please contact us with your thoughts about *The Soul Diet: Ten Steps towards Metaphysical Health*. Feel free to speak your mind or ask any questions. Examples of questions you could address:

- **Did this book challenge you and why?**
- **What did you learn from this book?**
- **Do you feel you would want to try this diet?**
- **Would you recommend this diet to others?**

Please indicate your consent for your comments to be used as possible blurbs or testimonials for this book.

It would be great to hear from you. The author is available for questions, interviews or speaking engagements.

Call directly: 206.721.1915
Fax: 206.721.1916
Email: info@NeemanHouse.com
Or write: Neeman House Publishers
                  5135 South Garden Street
                  Seattle, WA 98118
                  USA

Quick Order Form

Order more books for friends and colleagues on **SoulDiet.com** or with this form.

NOTE: **Free Shipping for orders of 2 or more books**
(Continental U.S. and Canada only)

☎ 206.721.1916. Fax this form

☎ Call **866.SOULDIET** (768.5343) toll free. Have your credit card ready.

🖱 email orders: **orders@neemanhouse.com**

✉ Neeman House Publishers, 5135 South Garden Street, Seattle, WA 98118

Please send _____ copy/ies of *The Soul Diet* at $24.95 U.S. (27.95 Can.) per copy

Please send FREE information on:

O workshops/speaking   O consulting/counseling   O forthcoming titles

_____
NAME

_____
ADDRESS

_____
CITY   STATE/PROVINCE   ZIP/POSTAL CODE

_____
PHONE

_____
EMAIL

SALES TAX: Please add 8.8% to total cost (books plus shipping) for orders shipped to Washington state addresses.

SHIPPING: $5.00 Continental U.S. (6.00 Can), but FREE for 2 or more books
Elsewhere: $10.00 for first book, $5.00 for each additional book

PAYMENT:
O Check enclosed
O Credit card: O Visa   O Master Card   O AMEX

_____
CARD NUMBER   EXP.DATE (MM/YY)